END OF AN ERA

The Rise and Fall of Solomon

JOHN MACARTHUR

THOMAS NELSON

Since 1798

Published in Nashville, Tennessee, by Thomas Nelson. Thomas Nelson is a trademark of Thomas Nelson, Inc.

Published in association with the literary agency of Wolgemuth & Associates, Inc.

Layout, design, and writing assistance by Gregory C. Benoit Publishing, Old Mystic, CT. ᏩB

Thomas Nelson, Inc. titles may be purchased in bulk for educational, business, fund-raising, or sales promotional use. For information, please e-mail *SpecialMarkets@ThomasNelson.com*.

ISBN 978-1-4185-3406-6

Printed in the United States of America

10 11 12 13 RRD 5 4 3 2

Contents

⁓ ◌ ⁓

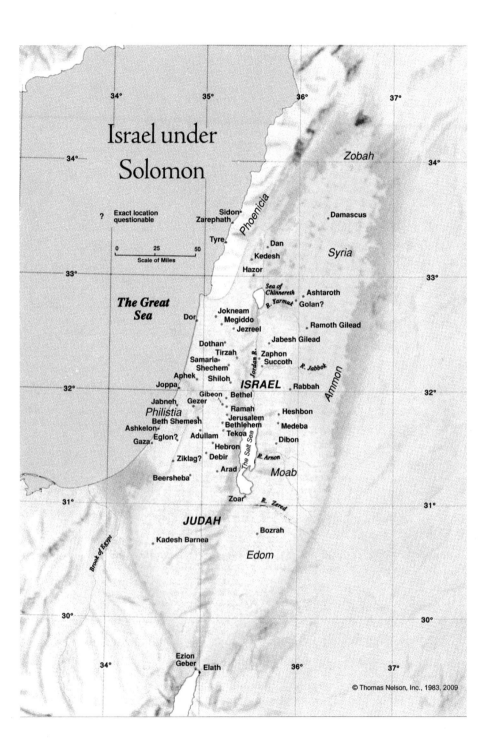

Israel under Solomon

Zobah

? Exact location questionable

0 25 50
Scale of Miles

Sidon
Zarephath
Tyre
Damascus

Phoenicia

Dan
Kedesh
Hazor

Syria

The Great Sea

Sea of Chinnereth
R. Yarmuk
Ashtaroth
Golan?

Jokneam
Dor
Megiddo
Jezreel
Ramoth Gilead

Dothan
Tirzah
Jabesh Gilead

Samaria
Shechem
Zaphon
Succoth
R. Jabbok

Jordan R.

Aphek
Shiloh
Joppa

ISRAEL
Rabbah

Ammon

Gibeon
Bethel
Jabneh
Gezer
Ramah
Heshbon

Philistia
Beth Shemesh
Jerusalem
Bethlehem
Medeba

Ashkelon
Eglon?
Adullam
Tekoa
Dibon

Gaza
Hebron
The Salt Sea

Ziklag?
Debir
R. Arnon

Arad
Moab

Beersheba

Zoar
R. Zered

JUDAH

Bozrah

Kadesh Barnea

Edom

Brook of Egypt

Ezion Geber
Elath

© Thomas Nelson, Inc., 1983, 2009

INTRODUCTION

Solomon was the son of King David and Queen Bathsheba. Though he was not the oldest of the king's sons, God had selected him to succeed his father to the throne of Israel. As he took on that task, he initially showed humility: when the Lord appeared to him in a dream and offered him anything he wanted, Solomon asked for wisdom. This priority pleased the Lord, and He gave him very great wisdom indeed, such that Solomon became renowned throughout the world as the wisest man who ever lived.

For the world, wisdom is the ability to live life with skill. It is associated with intelligence, power, and problem-solving. But in Scripture, true wisdom is not intellectual; it is moral. It is the ability to distinguish good from evil. Wisdom gives insight into the character of God, seen most clearly through the gospel. God is the sole source of true wisdom, and He gives it generously as a gift to anyone who asks. Yet in spite of the great value of wisdom, as well as its free availability, many people live their lives as fools. Why would anyone deliberately choose folly over wisdom? We will set out to find the answer in this study guide.

In these twelve studies, we will jump back and forth in chronological history, looking at one historical period and then skipping forward or backward in time as needed. We will examine the life of Solomon, and we will consider some other very memorable characters—including the wise woman and the foolish speaker. Through it all, we will learn some precious truths about the character of God, and we will see His great faithfulness in keeping His promises. We will learn, in short, what it means to walk by faith.

ᔐ WHAT WE'LL BE STUDYING ᔐ

This study guide is divided into four distinct sections in which we will examine selected Bible passages:

SECTION 1: HISTORY. In this first section, we will focus on the historical setting of our Bible text. These five lessons will give a broad overview of the people, places, and events that are important to this study. They will also provide the background for the next two sections. This is our most purely historical segment, focusing simply on what happened and why.

SECTION 2: CHARACTERS. The four lessons in this section will give us an opportunity to zoom in on the characters from our Scripture passages. Some of these people were introduced in section 1, but in this part of the study guide we will take a much closer look at these personalities. Why did God see fit to include them in His Book in the first place? What made them unique? What can we learn from their lives? In this practical section, we will answer all of these questions and more, as we learn how to live wisely by emulating the wisdom of those who came before us.

SECTION 3: THEMES. Section 3 consists of two lessons in which we will consider some of the broader themes and doctrines touched on in our selected Scripture passages. This is the guide's most abstract portion, wherein we will ponder specific doctrinal and theological questions that are important to the church today. As we ask what these truths mean to us as Christians, we will also look for practical ways to base our lives upon God's truth.

SECTION 4: SUMMARY AND REVIEW. In our final section, we will look back at the principles that we have discovered in the scriptures throughout this study guide. These will be our "takeaway" principles, those which permeate the Bible passages that we have studied. As always, we will be looking for ways to make these truths a part of our everyday lives.

⌁ ABOUT THE LESSONS ⌁

⊰ Each study begins with an introduction that provides the background for the selected Scripture passages.

⊰ To assist you in your reading, a section of notes—a miniature Bible commentary of sorts—offers both cultural information and additional insights.

⊰ A series of questions is provided to help you dig a bit deeper into the Bible text.

⊰ Overriding principles brought to light by the Bible text will be studied in each lesson. These principles summarize a variety of doctrines and practical truths found throughout the Bible.

⊰ Finally, additional questions will help you mine the deep riches of God's Word and, most importantly, to apply those truths to your own life.

Section 1:

History

In This Section:

THE RISE OF SOLOMON

1 KINGS 3, 4

✍ HISTORICAL BACKGROUND ✍

Solomon was the son of David, the second born to him through Bathsheba. David's relationship with Bathsheba did not begin nobly. She was married to another man when David called her to his palace, committed adultery with her, and got her pregnant. David then had her husband murdered in hopes of covering up his sin, and Bathsheba was silent about the entire affair. Thus, Solomon was the product of this illegal and immoral union.

One might expect that the son of David and Bathsheba would not make a very wise king, given this family background. Yet Solomon became the wisest man who ever lived, and people from all over the world traveled to Jerusalem to learn from him. This demonstrates that wisdom is not based upon one's upbringing or background or even one's resources. Wisdom is available to all people, regardless of their inherent skills or gifts, because it is a gift from God—and it is freely available to anyone who asks for it.

When Solomon took the throne in place of his father, he began his reign on a very good footing: he asked the Lord to give him wisdom to shepherd the people of God. The Lord answered Solomon's prayer, giving him not only wisdom, but also great riches and power. His kingdom grew to be one of the most powerful in the world at the time. Yes, Solomon began his reign very well—but we will soon discover that, in time, he set himself up for disaster.

✍ READING 1 KINGS 3:1–28 ✍

THE REIGN OF SOLOMON: *Solomon was the son of King David and Bathsheba. (See the previous book in this series,* Restoration of a Sinner, *for more background on David and Bathsheba). He was not David's eldest son, but he was the man whom God selected to lead His people.*

1. MARRIED PHARAOH'S DAUGHTER: This political alliance demonstrated how powerful and influential Israel was becoming at the time, since Egypt (a world superpower in its day) did not ordinarily make such alliances. Pharaoh's daughter was the most politically significant of Solomon's seven hundred wives (1 Kings 7:8; 9:16; 11:1). The Lord, however, had expressly forbidden His people to intermarry with the pagan nations (Deuteronomy 7), warning them that such marriages would lead the people astray. We will see in the next study that this was indeed the result.

THE CITY OF DAVID: That is, Jerusalem.

2. THE HIGH PLACES: The Canaanites worshiped their gods on hilltops, frequently in open-air shrines. The Israelites were commanded to destroy the altars that these pagans built there (Deuteronomy 7), and after the temple was completed, God's people were forbidden to use the sites at all. But they didn't listen, and their disobedience eventually led Israel into *syncretism*, the act of combining pagan practices with God's ordained worship.

A BLANK CHECK: *The Lord appears to Solomon in a dream and offers to give him anything he desires. Solomon's request may surprise you.*

3. SOLOMON LOVED THE LORD: Solomon began well, loving the Lord and following his father's example of walking according to God's Word. He sincerely desired to be faithful to the Lord and to be a good king, as David had been for most of his reign.

EXCEPT: This dangerous little word alerts us to Solomon's area of weakness. These "high places," even if they were now dedicated to worship of the Lord, may have been the former sites of Baal worship. At the very least, they were an example of God's people imitating the ways of the world, worshipping Him at places of convenience rather than in the tabernacle or the temple.

4. GIBEON: A hill approximately six miles northwest of Jerusalem. (See the map in the Introduction.)

5. WHAT SHALL I GIVE YOU?: Solomon received a unique offer from the Lord, permitting him to ask for anything he desired. In this, the Lord was also testing Solomon's heart to discover his deepest priorities. In spite of David's onetime adultery, he had been a man after God's own heart (see 1 Samuel 13:14 and Acts 13:22). Now here was Solomon's opportunity to demonstrate that he intended to follow his father's footsteps.

7. I AM A LITTLE CHILD: Solomon was probably about twenty years old when he assumed the throne. His answer to the Lord demonstrated a wholesome humility, as he recognized that it was a huge responsibility to lead the Lord's people. At this point in his life, he acknowledged his own limitations and understood that he could not hope to shepherd Israel under his own power. He needed God's help.

8. IN THE MIDST OF YOUR PEOPLE: Solomon underscored the fact that Israel was the Lord's nation, not his own. He recognized that he was accountable to God for the welfare of His people, and that realization was sobering.

9. AN UNDERSTANDING HEART: The Hebrew word translated *understanding* literally means "to hear, listen to, obey." Solomon very wisely asked the Lord to give him a listening and obedient heart that was turned fully toward the Word of God.

A GOOD CHOICE: *Solomon's request pleases the Lord, and He grants wisdom in abundance—along with things that Solomon didn't ask for.*

10. THE SPEECH PLEASED THE LORD: Christians would do well to imitate Solomon's example, asking the Lord to give them a hunger to understand and obey His Word. A heart for God is a gift from Him; it is not something that a person can attain by sheer willpower. But today, we have the presence of the Holy Spirit in our lives, and He is eager to give us this very thing.

11. LONG LIFE . . . RICHES . . . THE LIFE OF YOUR ENEMIES: Requests such as these are more typical of what a person might ask if given such carte blanche by the Lord—yet these things reflect the wisdom of the world, not the wisdom of God. We will contrast these two types of wisdom throughout these studies.

12. THERE HAS NOT BEEN ANYONE LIKE YOU: Solomon's great understanding enabled him to write the bulk of what is known as the "Wisdom Literature" (Proverbs, Ecclesiastes, and the Song of Solomon). This study will examine some of those writings.

13. I HAVE ALSO GIVEN YOU WHAT YOU HAVE NOT ASKED: Solomon asked for wisdom and understanding, and the Lord granted his request in superabundance. This is the way God loves to give to His people. As James reminds us, "If any of you lacks wisdom, let him ask of God, who gives to all liberally and without reproach, and it will be given to him" (James 1:5).

14. IF YOU WALK IN MY WAYS: God gave Solomon great wisdom as an unconditional gift, but He placed conditions on His offer of long life. Unfortunately, as we will see in the next study, Solomon did not meet those conditions and died before reaching seventy—a relatively young age in Solomon's day.

WISDOM IN PRACTICE: *Two prostitutes come to Solomon with a very difficult case. There are no witnesses, and it will require great wisdom to discern the truth.*

16. HARLOTS: It seems surprising to discover two prostitutes standing before the greatest king of the age, pleading their private cases, but this demonstrates that Solomon made himself available to people of all types within his kingdom. His wisdom and justice were accessible to all.

23. THE ONE SAYS . . . AND THE OTHER SAYS: The difficulty of this case was that there were no witnesses to corroborate one woman's story over the other—it was a matter of choosing which one to believe, and neither prostitute would have been considered a reliable witness.

25. DIVIDE THE LIVING CHILD IN TWO: In great wisdom, Solomon bypassed the conflicting claims of the two women and searched their hearts for the truth. He knew that the child's real mother would never permit such a horrible fate.

✣ READING 1 KINGS 4:29–34 ✣

WISER THAN ALL MEN: *God has granted Solomon's request to such a generous degree that his wisdom is greater than all men of his age.*

29. LARGENESS OF HEART: The Lord gave Solomon a great capacity for learning and understanding in a breadth of areas, including trees, animals, and fish (v. 33)—as well as the things of God. Solomon grew to be a man of immense learning.

31. HE WAS WISER THAN ALL MEN: God gifted Solomon so generously that he became wiser than anyone else of his age. The good news for us is that God has not changed—He is just as eager to give wisdom to men and women today as He was in Solomon's day. All we need to do is ask.

✣ FIRST IMPRESSIONS ✣

1. *Why did Solomon ask for wisdom instead of power or wealth or freedom from enemies? Why did God grant his request so generously?*

2. *If God appeared to you in a dream and offered you anything you wanted, what would you ask for?*

3. *Why did God make this amazing offer to Solomon? What does this reveal about His character?*

4. *If you had been in Solomon's place, how would you have dealt with the two prostitutes? How did Solomon's judgment demonstrate wisdom?*

↳ Some Key Principles ↵

Wisdom is moral, not merely intellectual.

When the Bible speaks of wisdom, it is not talking about a person's IQ. From God's perspective, wisdom is a moral quality. The wise person lives life skillfully because he has discernment and can distinguish between good and evil. A person can be a mathematical genius or a scholar of the highest degree and yet still be considered a fool if he does not understand the truths of Scripture. You can be a smart fool, but you cannot be a wise atheist.

Wisdom has nothing to do with a person's inherent intelligence or natural gifts. It is not gained through a good education; neither is it more available to certain social classes or income brackets. Wisdom comes only from God, and it is a gift He gives to those who *ask* for it. Solomon described wisdom and understanding as "more precious than rubies" (Proverbs 3:15). Nothing we desire can ever compare with wisdom, "for her proceeds are better than the profits of silver" (v. 14). Wisdom can bring long life, riches, and great honor, and it enables a person to live a peaceable and pleasant life (v. 16–17).

The Word of God contains the words of life, and they are a treasure beyond anything the world has to offer. "More to be desired are they than gold," wrote David, "yea, than much fine gold; sweeter also than honey and the honeycomb. Moreover by them Your servant is warned, and in keeping them there is great reward" (Psalm 19:10–11).

Wisdom comes through God's Word, and He gives it to us freely—if we ask.

Wisdom is seen in having the mind of Christ (see 1 Corinthians 2:16). When a person is wise, they see a situation as Christ would see it. This wisdom, of course, only comes through God's Word, and God Himself has promised to give understanding to anyone who will ask for it (James 1:5).

That does not mean that a person is uninvolved in gaining wisdom; it is an active skill, one that requires practice to grow and mature. But wisdom is available to anyone who desires it, and it is a free gift. What's more, it's a gift that God is eager to bestow on all His children, and He's always ready to give more whenever we ask. As James tells us, "If any of you lacks wisdom, let him ask of God, who gives to all liberally and without reproach, and it will be given to him" (James 1:5). Solomon asked the Lord for wisdom, and He gave it to him in abundance. Today, God's wisdom does not come in the form of a dream, but it comes through the gospel. First Corinthians 1:24 calls Christ "the wisdom of God," and Colossians 3:16 says that this wisdom is gained through the study of "the word of Christ." God is eager to bestow wisdom on us, and that wisdom is found in the pages of Scripture.

The more we obey God's Word, the deeper our love grows for Him.

As a young man, Solomon loved the Lord deeply and wanted to be obedient to His Word. In this, he was like his father, David, who made it a lifelong priority to follow God's law. Unfortunately, Solomon laid a trap for himself early in his kingship by mixing pagan practices into his worship, sacrificing to the Lord on the hilltops where the Canaanites had formerly worshiped the false god Baal.

Over the course of his lifetime, Solomon's love for the Lord grew lukewarm, as we will see in our next study. In contrast, David's love for God grew stronger and deeper the longer he walked in obedience. The difference is that David repented of his sinful behaviors, while Solomon continued to excuse them.

When we obey God, we give Him the opportunity to demonstrate His faithfulness, power, and love in our lives. We gain a deeper understanding of His character as we walk in obedience, and this leads to a deeper love for Him. As we will see in the life of Solomon, however, the opposite is also true: if we persist in ignoring His Word, our hearts can grow cold toward God.

ᕂ Digging Deeper ᕂ

5. *Define wisdom and understanding in your own words, giving practical examples of each.*

6. *Why was God so pleased with Solomon's request? Why did He give him so many other things as well? What does this suggest about the relationship between wisdom and riches?*

7. *In what ways are wisdom and understanding more valuable than anything the world can offer?*

8. What role does obedience play in gaining wisdom? How are wisdom and obedience inseparably linked?

↶ Taking It Personally ↷

9. In what areas of your life do you require wisdom at present? Take time right now to ask the Lord to give you wisdom in addressing those issues.

10. What things are most important to you? What are you striving for most actively: success? wealth? wisdom? understanding?

～ 2 ～
THE DECLINE OF SOLOMON

⋋ HISTORICAL BACKGROUND ⋌

Solomon began his reign on a high note, as we saw in our last study. He loved the Lord and walked according to His statutes, just as his father David had done—with one exception: he continued to offer sacrifices at the "high places," hilltops where the Canaanites had worshiped their false gods in the past.

Perhaps Solomon justified the practice in his own mind because it seemed expedient at the time. After all, it would be years before he would complete the temple in Jerusalem, so it might have seemed more important to continue worshipping the Lord than to worry about the details. But this disobedience laid the foundation for future rule-breaking in ways that eventually led to his downfall.

The root of Solomon's syncretism was his marriages; Solomon married a great multitude of women, and he had a thousand wives before he was finished. Many of these women were foreigners from political marriages that ensured peace with neighboring nations. This, too, may have seemed expedient to him at the time, since such unions were common in the world of Solomon's day. Solomon might have told himself that mixed marriages were just part of being king, a political leader dealing with the realities of the world around him. But these wives captured his heart. Solomon loved them more than he loved God, and thus he allowed the high places to continue.

The Lord had forbidden His people to intermarry with the world around them, because mixed marriages would lead Israel into idolatry. And this is exactly what happened to Solomon—even the wisest man in the world is not exempt from obeying the Word of God.

⋋ READING 1 KINGS 11:1–43 ⋌

SOLOMON'S WIVES: *King Solomon marries a thousand wives and concubines, many of whom are from foreign nations. This is in violation of the Lord's commands.*

1. King Solomon loved many foreign women: Solomon violated God's law in two ways: he took many wives (Deuteronomy 17:17), and he married foreign women (Deuteronomy 7:1–4). The Lord had expressly warned the Israelites not to marry the Canaanites because such unions would lead His people into paganism. This was precisely the case with Solomon. Many of his marriages were probably political arrangements, intended to secure peace treaties with neighboring nations, but Solomon's pragmatism in such matters still led to defiance to the Word of God.

Moabites, Ammonites, Edomites, Sidonians, and Hittites: The Moabites and Ammonites were descendants of Lot (Genesis 19:36–38), while the Edomites were the offspring of Esau (Genesis 36:1). The Sidonians lived in Sidon, on the shore of the Mediterranean, and the Hittites were spread throughout Syria. (See the map in the Introduction.)

2. You shall not intermarry with them: The Lord had warned His people not to intermarry with the Gentiles because it would make them "unequally yoked"— that is, the Israelites were God's people, while the Gentiles in Canaan served false gods, so the married couple would be yoked to different masters. This same principle applies to Christians today: we are warned in Scripture not to marry nonbelievers, because the nonbeliever will lead the believer away from God (2 Corinthians 6:14).

Surely they will turn away your hearts after their gods: Some Christians excuse romantic involvement with non-Christians with the argument that they will lead the other person to the Lord. But God warned the people here very clearly that it does not work that way. When a Christian is unequally yoked with a non-Christian, the Christian's walk with the Lord generally will suffer.

Solomon clung to these in love: Solomon was the wisest man who ever lived, yet his great wisdom did not prevent him from being led away from the Lord by his pagan wives—even though he may have loved them dearly and would certainly have wanted the best for them.

4. the heart of his father David: Obviously, David did not lead a sinless life. The difference between David and Solomon was in their responses to sin: David repented and turned his life back to the Lord, while Solomon persisted in his disobedience.

Syncretism: *Solomon's wives lead him away from the Lord's prescribed worship, and he adds in elements of pagan religions.*

5. Ashtoreth . . . Milcom: Ashtoreth was the Canaanite goddess of love and fertility. Milcom was also called Molech, whose worship practices included child sacrifice. There is a certain irony in the fact that Solomon's wives, whom he loved, led him to worship the pagan goddess of love. The child sacrifice of Molech typified the fact that Solomon, as the shepherd of God's people, led Israel away from the Lord and into the arms of foreign gods.

6. DID NOT FULLY FOLLOW THE LORD: It is noteworthy that Solomon followed the Lord partially, but not fully. He did obey the Lord's Word in some aspects, such as building the temple, yet he also indulged disobedience in other areas. The result of this partial obedience was disastrous. The Lord calls His people to complete obedience; He does not give us leeway to pick and choose what parts of His Word we will follow.

7. SOLOMON BUILT A HIGH PLACE: Here we see the fruit of Solomon's earlier failure to remove the high places of worship. His partial compliance with God's will early in his life led to total noncompliance later.

CHEMOSH: A Moabite deity that required child sacrifice.

GOD REJECTS SOLOMON AS KING: *The Lord will not permit the shepherd of His people to adulterate His Word with pagan practices.*

9. THE LORD BECAME ANGRY WITH SOLOMON: God had given Solomon great wisdom, as well as riches and power—but these gifts did not exempt him from walking in obedience. Quite the contrary, in fact: the Lord's great generosity made Solomon all the more accountable to God's commands. The Lord does not pick favorites; all men are called to obey His Word, from the king to the poorest peasant.

11. I WILL SURELY TEAR THE KINGDOM AWAY FROM YOU: The Lord had given Solomon great gifts, but those gifts were for the purpose of ruling His people, not for Solomon's selfish use. Solomon had led God's people astray, so the Lord would take away his throne, removing his descendants from leadership over His people.

12. FOR THE SAKE OF YOUR FATHER DAVID: The Lord had made an unconditional covenant with David, establishing his throne forever (2 Samuel 7:12–16). It was through this covenant that God would eventually establish the reign of His Son, Jesus. The Lord had also promised David that He would not remove His mercy from his son, as He had from Saul, effectively promising that He would not expel Solomon from the throne. Nevertheless, Solomon's dynasty would end when he died.

13. I WILL GIVE ONE TRIBE TO YOUR SON: The tribe of Judah remained loyal to the house of David. The Lord was telling Solomon that a great division was coming to Israel, when the nation would split in two.

15. WHEN DAVID WAS IN EDOM: The Lord had given David many great victories over Israel's enemies, including the Edomites. (See 2 Samuel 8 for details.)

26. Jeroboam: The Lord raised up Jeroboam to tear ten tribes of Israel away from Solomon, thus dividing the nation. He became the first king of the northern tribes, which continued to be called Israel, while Solomon's son Rehoboam took the throne in Judah after his father's death.

40. Solomon therefore sought to kill Jeroboam: The end of Solomon's reign bore a striking similarity to that of Saul. Both kings had been rejected by God, and when He selected the man who would be the next king, both Saul and Solomon responded by trying to murder the Lord's chosen one. That Solomon would try to kill the Lord's anointed successor demonstrated how far his heart had strayed from God.

⤙ First Impressions ⤚

1. *What might have been Solomon's reasons for marrying so many women? How might he have justified it in his own mind?*

2. *What role did Solomon's marriages play in his downfall? How might his life have ended differently if he had not married foreigners?*

3. Why did God become angry with Solomon? What specifically had Solomon done wrong?

4. Why is it dangerous for a Christian to marry a non-Christian? What causes the Christian to be led astray by the non-Christian, rather than vice versa?

☙ Some Key Principles ❧

Christians should not marry non-Christians.

God warned His people repeatedly in the Old Testament not to marry those who did not obey His Word. He had specifically advised the Israelites as they were leaving Egypt not to give their sons and daughters to the people of Canaan, because those people worshiped false idols rather than the true God (Deuteronomy 7:1–3).

The primary reason for these injunctions was that such marriages would cause God's people to drift away from obedience and into idolatry. Christians today sometimes argue that they can lead a non-Christian spouse to salvation, using that logic to justify an unequal union. Such thinking is misguided, however, for God's Word warns consistently that the opposite will prove true: the unbeliever will lead the believer away from God (Exodus 34:12–16).

The Bible uses the metaphor of two oxen sharing a yoke as they pull a plow. A Christian marrying a non-Christian is like yoking two animals together who want to pull in opposite directions—and such an arrangement can only lead to disaster. Paul cautioned, "Do not be unequally yoked together with unbelievers. For what fellowship has righteousness with lawlessness? And what communion has light with darkness? And what accord has Christ with Belial? Or what part has a believer with an unbeliever?" (2 Corinthians 6:14–15). God's people must not intermarry with those who are not part of His body.

God calls His people to complete—not partial—obedience.

Solomon began well. He loved God and followed His laws, just as his father had done, we are told in 1 Kings 3:3. But that verse has one small word that we must not overlook: *except.* "And Solomon loved the LORD, walking in the statutes of his father David, *except* that he sacrificed and burned incense at the high places." As we mentioned in Study 1, Solomon laid a trap for himself early on in his life, and in this study we have seen the terrible fruit of his decision.

The problem was that Solomon compromised by thinking that there was an area of his life that was somehow exempt from obedience to the Lord's statutes. God's people ⌐ot to offer sacrifice on the high places—their worship was to be conducted at the ⌐usalem. Yet Solomon did not follow that principle, continuing to offer sac- ⌐d once been used to worship pagan gods. He also failed to obey the ⌐marrying foreign women, and when he grew older, these areas of disobedience turned his heart away from serving God: "his heart was not loyal to the LORD his God, as was the heart of his father David" (1 Kings 11:4).

Walking with the Lord requires obedience on our part, and we are not given the freedom to handpick which areas of His Word we will obey and which we will ignore. It is *all* for our good. "For the word of God is living and powerful, and sharper than any two-edged sword, piercing even to the division of soul and spirit, and of joints and marrow, and is a discerner of the thoughts and intents of the heart. And there is no creature hidden from His sight, but all things are naked and open to the eyes of Him to whom we must give account" (Hebrews 4:12–13). Paul told Timothy, "All Scripture is given by inspiration of God, and is profitable for doctrine, for reproof, for correction, for instruction in righteousness, that the man of God may be complete, thoroughly equipped for every good work" (2 Timothy 3:16–17).

The Lord does not tolerate syncretism.

Syncretism is the act of combining elements of diverse religious philosophies into a new form of worship. Solomon attempted to do this when he added pagan practices to the prescribed worship of God, drawing in elements from the worship of a wide variety of false gods. The Lord had expressly forbidden His people from intermarrying for that very reason, and Solomon's paganism led to the loss of his kingdom.

The modern church has frequently fallen into syncretism as well, incorporating worldly principles and ideas into the Word of God. This can be seen in the addition of New Age ideas, evolutionary thinking, self-help approaches to sinful behaviors, or pandering to cultural trends. Christians are very unwise when they attempt to add to the written Word of God, because it is complete already, as pertinent today as when it was written.

As we will see in the course of these studies, the world offers a form of wisdom that can appear sound at first glance, but its source is not from God. This "wisdom" is from below, not from above. Christians must be constantly on guard to prevent such false wisdom from being added to the sound teachings of Scripture.

⌒ DIGGING DEEPER ⌒

5. What worldly teachings or philosophies have found their way into church practices today?

6. Solomon evidently genuinely loved his wives. Why was that tenderness not enough to prevent him from going astray? How does this principle apply in modern times?

7. How does the injunction against unequal yoking apply to other relationships besides marriage, such as friendships, church membership, business dealings, etc.?

8. How does a Christian reach out to the unsaved while avoiding unequal yoking? How is this balance achieved?

9. Are there areas in your life where you are not walking in complete obedience? What will you do this week to change that?

10. Are there people in your life who are leading you away from a close walk with God? What will you do about those relationships?

⟨ 3 ⟩

A Time for Everything

↬ Historical Background ↫

God gave Solomon great wisdom, as we saw in Study 1, to the point that he was deemed the wisest man of all time. But what would he do with that wisdom? He could use it to lead a life that glorified God or he could abuse it in a quest to find satisfaction apart from God. We will see that, despite his wisdom, Solomon did not love the Lord with his whole heart. He filled his life with compromises; whom he married, how he worshiped, and what he valued in life was corrupted by his quest for meaning apart from God.

As he grew older, Solomon became cynical and despondent. He was fabulously wealthy and enjoyed great power and prestige in the world of his day. This permitted him whatever indulgence of the flesh he desired, and he sampled all that the world had to offer. But when he looked back on his life, he saw that all the world's offerings led only to emptiness, and he declared that life itself was nothing but vanity.

The book of Ecclesiastes encompasses Solomon's conclusions on the meaning of life. Because of this, it is a very profound book. If it is only given a surface reading, it could seem depressing, with its repeated refrain of "'Vanity of vanities,' says the Preacher, 'All is vanity'" (Ecclesiastes 12:8; see also 1:2). But Solomon's point is that the riches of the world, the sexual pleasure found in a thousand different women, and the power invested in the king are all unable to give any kind of eternal meaning to life. Thus, Ecclesiastes actually offers both a warning and an encouragement: it warns against pursuing the emptiness of the world, and it encourages trusting that God is sovereign over all life's events.

There is a time for everything, Solomon writes, but we must always remember that our times are in God's hands. When we order our lives according to an understanding of His sovereignty, we gain an eternal perspective—and we avoid a life built on the vanity of vanities.

✑ Reading Ecclesiastes 3:1–22 ✑

A Time for Every Purpose: *God appoints "seasons" and "times" for every activity on earth. This passage is a testimony to God's complete sovereignty over every conceivable event in human life. But it also shows that while earthly pursuits are good in their proper place and time, they are unprofitable when pursued as source of joy in life.*

1. A time for every purpose: This chapter lists many facets of human life, and in most cases a person finds times and seasons that call for one or another of these endeavors. But Solomon's larger point is that God has a time and a season for all things according to His purposes, and He unfailingly turns everything to further those purposes. This chapter underscores the sovereignty of God as well as the futility of human endeavor apart from God. People may do this or that, but they can only do so in the time appointed by God.

2. born . . . die: Solomon grouped pairs of opposites throughout this list of life's events, beginning with the most inevitable of all human experiences: birth and death. This also underscores the fact that Solomon was describing life in a fallen world, rather than the world as God originally intended it. Death entered the world through Adam's sin (Romans 5:12), and ever since that day, life has included frustration, struggle, and sorrows for the human race (Genesis 3)—yet this was not what God originally intended.

plant . . . pluck: Human life may include many forms of sorrow and hardship, yet the hand of God is always visible to those willing to see it. He continues to maintain the seasons and cycles that He instituted at Creation, including the times of planting and harvest. God's sovereignty sustains all life on earth.

3. kill . . . heal: God instituted human government after the great flood, and charged Noah's descendants with the responsibility of protecting human life by putting murderers to death (Genesis 9:6). The Lord's sovereign hand does bring judgment and death, but it also brings life and healing.

break down . . . build up: God's supreme purposes sometimes involve tearing down the works of men, and other times building up things that will last into eternity. The Lord tore down the walls of Jericho, but He established a kingdom in the line of David that will last forever through Jesus Christ.

4. weep . . . laugh . . . mourn . . . dance: The normal cycle of human emotion is common to all people, as good times and hard times come upon all men. Yet the hand of God is in control of all such events, whether or not we are aware of it at the time. Weeping and laughing may be private expressions of the conditions of our lives, while mourning and dancing are more public expressions.

BUILDING AND MENDING: *Solomon now turns to the issues involved in our daily labors—farming, homemaking, even finances.*

5. CAST AWAY STONES: Stones were "cast away" during times of peace and safety, as farmers would clear fields to make them usable for planting or grazing. Gathering stones together might imply a time of battle, or even a time of judgment, as stones could be used in warfare or in a public execution.

REFRAIN FROM EMBRACING: The embrace spoken of here implies sexual intimacy. God's Word makes clear stipulations concerning the sexual embrace, and it is only appropriate within the context of marriage.

6. GAIN . . . LOSE: Here is another experience common to all people, as most of us experience times both of prosperity and of lack. Once again, God oversees all such cycles, whether or not we recognize His hand in the process.

KEEP . . . THROW AWAY: As with the cycles of economy, most people also experience times of acquiring and times of letting go of material possessions.

7. TEAR . . . SEW: People in Bibles times would frequently tear their garments when they heard tragic news, as an outward sign of deep grief, whereas sewing garments together would indicate a more peaceful time of life. The Lord also speaks in Scripture of tearing and mending; as we saw in our last study, the Lord promised that He would "tear the kingdom away" from Solomon (1 Kings 11:11).

KEEP SILENCE . . . SPEAK: Solomon wrote many proverbs concerning what times are appropriate for speech or silence, and we will consider these in Study 7.

LOVE . . . HATE: It may seem incongruous that God would deem hate appropriate at certain times, yet He Himself hates sin. In the book of Revelation, the Lord speaks of hating certain false doctrines and commends those believers who share His animosity for them (2:6).

9. WHAT PROFIT HAS THE WORKER: Solomon's overall point in this chapter was that man's labors have no lasting profit in themselves, for one's best efforts are worthless apart from God. This was not a dark cynicism, as some have suggested; on the contrary, a person's work can be profitable when it is done under the Lord's guiding hand. God is sovereign over all things, and the person who submits to His sovereignty will discover that his labors are not in vain.

WHERE GOD FITS IN: *Solomon now turns his eyes heavenward and considers the role that God plays in man's daily affairs.*

10. THE GOD-GIVEN TASK: Without God's involvement, all of life would be merely a meaningless cycle of birth and death, pleasure and pain, success and failure. But when we see that God's hand rules purposefully over all events, we discover that there is a way to live with meaning and purpose.

11. HE HAS MADE EVERYTHING BEAUTIFUL IN ITS TIME: God's self-governing hand guides all our events, and the Lord never does anything that is ugly or evil. Therefore, the Christian can rest in the knowledge that He will use every event of our lives to produce His will, and He will bring beauty even out of ugliness and sorrow. The key here is the fact that He will do so in His time, not according to our schedule.

HE HAS PUT ETERNITY IN THEIR HEARTS: The first part of this chapter was concerned with the events of life, those temporal things that come into everyone's life. But God is concerned with eternity, and He uses temporal events to further His eternal plan and kingdom. People were created for God's eternal purposes, and it is part of our nature to long for those things that transcend our lives on earth. This is the very reason people can become cynical and desperate when they don't have a relationship with God: they long for eternity, yet all they see are the apparently random cycles of life on earth. God has "put eternity in their hearts" so they might recognize that there is more to life than that which is of this world.

NO ONE CAN FIND OUT THE WORK THAT GOD DOES: God's nature is beyond the comprehension of men. The Bible tells us that He is sovereign over all things, that He orders the times and events of our lives, and that He uses everything—both good and evil—to further His plans. We cannot hope to understand His purposes for every event of our lives; we must learn to trust that He is in control, and that He is faithful to turn all things to His glory.

13. IT IS THE GIFT OF GOD: The key to contentment in life is to remember that all things come into our lives from the hand of God, both pleasure and pain. God's gift does not lie so much in the event itself, but in the eternal good that He will bring forth from it. Even a rich man cannot find long-term satisfaction from his wealth, because his profit is limited to this world. God brings eternal profit to His children, and He does so through our failures as well as our successes.

ALL IS VANITY: *The term vanity expresses the futile attempt to be satisfied apart from God. Solomon concludes with the realization that all life ends in death, regardless of how one lives. Thus, the only thing that matters is the judgment of God.*

16. WICKEDNESS WAS THERE: When we view life from a human standpoint, we are likely to fall into hopeless pessimism because we see the injustice and wickedness in the world around us. Christians must remember that God is always in control, even when we see wickedness in the place of judgment and iniquity in the place of righteousness. Man sees only what is temporal, but God sees all things from an eternal point of view.

17. God shall judge: The unsaved do not acknowledge the fact that God will one day judge the living and the dead. The world teaches us that there are no eternal consequences to our actions, but God reminds His people that He will one day judge all men. This knowledge can also bring comfort to God's people, as we sometimes are called upon to endure the world's corruption of truth and justice.

19. Man has no advantage over animals: If a person tries to find meaning in life apart from God, his life will be as futile as an animal's, because death awaits them both. But unlike the animals, humans will live forever. So in that sense, a person who lives his life apart from God is actually *worse* off than an animal because at least animals escape judgment.

All is vanity: Again, this is the ultimate conclusion that unsaved people are forced to reach. If there were no God in control of men's eternal destiny, then all of life would be futile and vain.

ᕇ First Impressions ᕇ

1. *How do verses 1–10 make you feel? Do you react with discouragement, or do you feel encouraged by this passage?*

2. *Why did Solomon say that there is a time to hate? What might be some examples of godly hatred?*

3. How would you describe the theological truths in this passage?

4. When have you seen God make something beautiful out of an unpleasant situation? What unpleasant aspects of your situation today might He beautify in the future?

↳ Some Key Principles ↰

God is sovereign, and He uses every event of our lives for His purposes.

We live in a fallen world. God originally created the world without sin or death. But when Adam disobeyed God's command (Genesis 2–3), his sin brought the curse of death and sorrow upon the entire world. As a result, our lives are marked by times of suffering and grief, and ultimately everyone faces physical death.

God was not caught by surprise when Adam sinned; He designed the world in such a way that he would receive glory as the savior of mankind. He describes Jesus as "the lamb slain from the foundation of the world" (Revelation 13:8). Everything that exists, exists to bring glory to God, including our sin. When sin entered the world, life became meaningless unless, of course, a person is reconciled to God. Today, if a person has a relationship with God through Jesus Christ, everything becomes meaningful. There is nothing in life that falls outside the realm of God's control, and He uses all things to further His own timeless plan.

His plan for you includes making you more like His Son, Jesus, and He uses every event of your life to advance this cause—including events that may bring heartache for a time. It can be easy to forget this fact when we are faced with difficulty, yet we will find such times easier to endure if we rest in God's sovereignty. As Paul reminds us, "all things work together for good to those who love God, to those who are the called according to His purpose" (Romans 8:28).

The world's philosophies lead to cynicism and despair.

Secular science teaches that mankind evolved from nothing, and that there is no God who oversees and sustains the world. This teaching forces people to conclude that life's events are random; if there is no God in control of the world, then everything that happens is mere chance. If there is no judgment, then this life is all that matters, and if everyone dies, then this life does not matter that much anyway.

The false religions of the world teach that mankind can somehow overcome this empty cycle of life and death by his own efforts—by trusting in good works to escape judgment or by reincarnating again and again until he attains a sinless state. But such views lead only to despair, because no one can live a sinless life, and no one can ever hope to defeat death. People who strive to overcome the curse of death by their own labors will ultimately become hopeless and cynical, because they will discover that they are power-less to do so, yet they will not know the God who has already defeated death.

Christians, on the other hand, should never become cynical because we know that life is more than a terrestrial cycle of ups and downs. It is God who created all things, and He is in absolute control of every event of our lives. Nothing can separate us from the love of God, and this assurance will keep us from despair.

Keep your focus on eternity, not on the things of the world.

Solomon began his reign with great wisdom, but he gradually lost his focus, as we have seen in our previous studies. He lost sight of the eternal perspective and began to focus instead on the things of this world. As a result, he turned away from full obedience to God and followed after the empty practices of paganism.

The danger is that even Christians can lose their eternal focus, and the result is just as disastrous for us today as it was for Solomon many years ago. If we allow the world's values to creep into our thinking, we run the risk of losing sight of God's divine perspective—and this, as we have seen, leads only to despair.

We keep our focus on eternity by remembering that we will live forever, that this temporal life is just that—temporary. Times of prosperity can be just as misleading as times of suffering, for wealth and success can make us forget that the things of this world will pass away. John reflected this understanding when he wrote, "Do not love the world or the things in the world. If anyone loves the world, the love of the Father is not in him. For all that is in the world—the lust of the flesh, the lust of the eyes, and the pride of life—is not of the Father but is of the world" (1 John 2:15–16).

✌ Digging Deeper ✌

5. Why does Solomon say that there is "a time for every purpose"? What does this mean from God's eternal perspective?

6. What is each person's "God-given task"? What is your God-given task at present? How well are you fulfilling it?

7. What "season" are you in right now? How might God be using your circumstances to further His plan for your life?

8. List ways below that you have seen God's sovereignty in your life. How can these things encourage you to trust Him in the future?

9. *Where is your focus in life: on eternity, or on the world? What priorities might the Lord want you to change?*

10. *How do you respond to disappointment or hardship? Is your tendency toward cynicism or despair, or do you trust God to work things to His glory?*

~ 4 ~
THE FULL DUTY OF MAN

✎ HISTORICAL BACKGROUND ✎

Solomon grew to be a very wealthy and powerful king. Leaders from nations around the world came to him to learn from his wisdom and to marvel at his accomplishments. The temple and the palace that he built were considered wonders of the known world; he had a thousand wives and concubines; his army was the best equipped and most powerful on earth; he was the first leader to solidify control of the trade routes connecting Africa, Europe, and Asia. Solomon sampled all that the world had to offer, and there was no pursuit or pleasure that he denied himself.

Yet, near the end of his life, he declared solemnly that everything was empty. "Vanity of vanities," he declared repeatedly, "all is vanity." And he concluded that everything that is done under the sun is meaningless, because death comes to everyone in the end—regardless of how they live. This is the repetitious refrain in the book of Ecclesiastes; it is Solomon's final assessment of all his life's accomplishments and indulgences.

But there is a much deeper and more important theme running through Ecclesiastes, and it is a message of hope, not of despair. There is a way for a man or woman to live a fulfilling life, wrote Solomon: by living for the glory of God. That duty is succinctly summarized at the end of the book: fear God and keep His commandments. When Christians live with this injunction always in mind, they will avoid the pessimistic despair of a life of vanity.

✎ READING ECCLESIASTES 2:17–26 ✎

HATING LIFE: *Solomon opens this passage with a note of cynicism and hopelessness. What is the point of life's toil, he asks, if it all ends in death?*

17. I HATED LIFE: In the first half of this chapter, Solomon tested all that life had to offer: pleasure, work, pursuits of the flesh, and even human wisdom. (We will discuss the two types of wisdom in Study 11.) He had found them all empty and declared that all were mere vanity. He discovered that the world cannot offer anything of lasting worth, because everything on earth ends with death—and the same death comes upon the wise man and the fool.

UNDER THE SUN: The concept of "under the sun" is the important element in Solomon's pursuit of meaning. It indicates that he had been searching for a source of sustaining value in temporal areas, and he had found none. Under the sun, he had examined all that is available in earthly life, but all proved to be vain. Trying to find lasting significance apart from God is like "grasping for the wind."

18. THE MAN WHO WILL COME AFTER ME: It is futile to amass great wealth and power; even those who build great empires or extensive business monopolies will one day die, and their vast wealth and power will fall into the hands of someone else.

19. HE WILL RULE OVER ALL MY LABOR: The man who strives his whole life to acquire great wealth is merely doing all the hard work for someone else's benefit. The one who inherits that wealth may prove to be a fool, using his riches in ways that his predecessor never intended. This was literally true in Solomon's case because his son—Rehoboam—was a colossal fool who ruined the powerful empire that he inherited (1 Kings 12).

20. THE LABOR IN WHICH I HAD TOILED UNDER THE SUN: Solomon underscored the fact that all these pursuits were for things found *under* the sun. It is a vain pursuit to chase after prosperity and power, for they are of this world and will remain under the sun even after the one who acquired them has departed into eternity.

FINDING SATISFACTION IN LABOR: *One way that a man can find some solace in life is to delight himself in the work God gives him to do.*

23. HIS WORK BURDENSOME: Pursuit of worldly gain, of things found under the sun, is burdensome because one is always at risk of losing it all. This burden weighs heavily upon one's mind, to the point of making the weary soul lose sleep with worry. The more you have, the more you worry about losing it.

24. HIS SOUL SHOULD ENJOY GOOD IN HIS LABOR: Solomon acknowledged that even life's material blessings are from the hand of God, for He created all things to be good (Genesis 1:31). It is not wrong to enjoy the blessings of life, especially taking delight in the work that God provides; the problem comes when a person thinks that this enjoyment somehow gives meaning to his life. The fact is, it is meaningless in and of itself, but it can be a tool for deepening one's relationship with his Creator.

26. A MAN WHO IS GOOD IN HIS SIGHT: At the end of all his striving for meaning, Solomon returned to the realization that God's perspective is the only truth in this world. The world might declare that a man is good and wise if he acquires great wealth or produces impressive works, but that is not God's view. Someone who is good in God's sight is a person "after His own heart," one who builds his life on the Word of God (Acts 13:22).

⤳ READING ECCLESIASTES 9:1–5 ⤳

BUT DEATH STILL COMES: *Even when we find satisfaction in work, Solomon continues, death still ends it all. Every living thing in this world ends the same way.*

1. THEIR WORKS ARE IN THE HAND OF GOD: God is completely sovereign over all the affairs of men. In this passage, Solomon demonstrated that the same result comes to all men, both righteous and unrighteous, when looked at from a temporal perspective. But God sees all things from an eternal perspective, and the eternal outcome of a person's life may be very different from his outcome on this fallen planet.

PEOPLE KNOW NEITHER LOVE NOR HATRED: That is, mankind can only see what is present and past, not what awaits them in the future. No matter what success or failure a person has experienced in his life, he cannot predict what God will do tomorrow. Man is given work to do, but God controls the results.

2. ONE EVENT HAPPENS TO THE RIGHTEOUS AND THE WICKED: Death comes to all men equally, regardless of how they have lived their lives. Furthermore, death ends the labors and deeds of each person, and no one can carry any secular accomplishments into eternity. The truly wise person will lay up for himself sacred treasure—in heaven—that will last forever (Matthew 6:19–20).

4. A LIVING DOG IS BETTER THAN A DEAD LION: This proverb reflects the characteristic wisdom of man, pointing out that even the lowliest creature is better off alive than the most noble creature is dead. There is truth in this on a temporal level, but it suggests that death is the end of human existence—and that is not the case. In the eternal perspective, the righteous are better off than the wicked, whether dead or alive.

5. THE DEAD KNOW NOTHING: This again reflects the wisdom of men, that a man's labors end with the grave. Conversely, God's wisdom teaches us that our labors on earth can bring us eternal rewards.

THEY HAVE NO MORE REWARD: The wise man, therefore, will use his time on earth to lay up eternal treasure. In this sense, it is true that a man's labors end with the grave, for after death no one has any further opportunity for eternal gain or loss—a man's decision is made when he dies, and he can never return to life to change his mind. Therefore, we must labor for the Lord while we have the opportunity, since death awaits us all (John 9:4).

⤙ Reading Ecclesiastes 12:13–14 ⤚

Fear and Obey God: *Solomon gives hope to his readers in his summarization of his answer to life's questions: fear God and obey His Word.*

13. THE CONCLUSION OF THE WHOLE MATTER: Solomon had explored everything that the world had to offer and had found it all to be vanity. At the end of his quest, he returned to the true wisdom of his youth, recognizing that lasting value and meaning can only be found in a relationship with God.

FEAR GOD AND KEEP HIS COMMANDMENTS: This summarizes the entire purpose of life from an eternal point of view. To "fear" God is to hold Him in reverence, to honor Him as Lord of all creation. Keeping His commandments does not necessarily preclude a person from enjoying work or finding delight in the life that God grants; in fact, the contrary is the case: the person who fears God and keeps His commandments will find true satisfaction and peace in life, because he knows that God is in control of all things.

14. GOD WILL BRING EVERY WORK INTO JUDGMENT: The wise man always remembers that judgment is coming. God will bring unbelievers into eternal judgment (Revelation 20:11–15). Christians will never face eternal judgment, yet we will face God's assessment of our lives, when He will test each believer's works to see whether they were for God's glory. That which is done for His glory will be like gold, silver, and precious stones, while that which we do for earthly gain will be burned up like wood, hay, and straw (1 Corinthians 3:10–15).

⤙ First Impressions ⤚

1. *Why did Solomon frequently repeat the phrase "under the sun"? What was he referring to? What did it reveal about his priorities?*

2. *What caused Solomon to find no value in his work? How can a person find joy in work?*

3. *What did Solomon mean when he said that "a living dog is better than a dead lion" (Ecclesiastes 9:4)? In what sense is this true? In what sense is it not true?*

4. *Why did Solomon declare that everything in life is vanity?*

ᔕ Some Key Principles ᔕ

Life is meaningless apart from God.

Solomon enjoyed unprecedented peace and success during his reign over Israel. He had fabulous wealth, far-reaching power, and best of all, the wisdom to use it well. Toward the end of his life, he reflected on the things that he had enjoyed, and he acknowledged that he had indulged in everything that the world had to offer: pleasure, wealth, creative works, fleshly pursuits, and everything else "under the sun." Yet, contrary to what the world would have us believe, he found it all to be pointless, the vanity of vanities.

Solomon's problem, as we saw in Study 2, was that he had departed from an obedient walk with God. He had abandoned the Source of wisdom and had begun seeking fulfillment in the things that the world has to offer. Yet for all his searching, he found nothing that could bring lasting satisfaction; all was vanity because the things he tried were devoid of God's blessing.

God wants His children to live fruitful and satisfying lives, although that also includes times of discipline and suffering. Satisfaction comes not from enjoying good things on earth, but from walking in a relationship with the Author of all that is good. Joy and meaning are found only in the Giver of good gifts, not in the gifts themselves. When we walk in obedience to God's Word, we find contentment with the lives that God gives us; apart from such obedience, however, even the best things of the world are empty and vain.

Store up treasure in heaven, not on earth.

When Solomon was a young man, the Lord offered him anything that he requested. He could have asked for a long life, great wealth, worldwide power and fame, or practically anything that a man could desire in this world. But instead he requested God's wisdom, that he might be able to rule over God's people well and be pleasing to the Lord. At that point in his life, Solomon had his eyes focused on eternity, and he was eager to lay up treasures in the kingdom of God.

As we have seen, however, he gradually took his eyes off of eternity and focused them on the things of earth—and the book of Ecclesiastes tells us the result of that focus: vanity of vanities. The trinkets and baubles of this world can seem very appealing to our fleshly eyes. But no worldly possession or accomplishment lasts forever; all temporal things are just that: temporal and temporary.

Human nature is such that we tend to keep our eyes focused on the things we value most, like a king watching over his vast treasure hoard. Wherever we place our treasure is exactly the point where we will fix our attention. But our true treasure lies in eternity, where we can never lose the things that God gives us. The Lord is faithful to reward those who serve Him, and those eternal rewards are the only things of lasting value. That's why Jesus said, "Do not lay up for yourselves treasures on earth, where moth and rust destroy and where thieves break in and steal; but lay up for yourselves treasures in heaven, where neither moth nor rust destroys and where thieves do not break in and steal. For where your treasure is, there your heart will be also" (Matthew 6:19–21).

The day of judgment is coming.

People who lay up treasure in this world alone do so in part because they have lost sight of eternity. The world teaches us that this life is all that matters, and more specifically, that there is no God to whom mankind will give an account. If there is no God, and this life is all that we get, then one might as well live as he chooses. This is at the root of the modern cult of self-love and self-esteem, as people today make pleasing themselves their sole aim.

But the Bible makes it very clear that God will one day judge the earth, and every person who has ever lived will stand before Him. Those who have rejected Christ as their Savior will face the dreadful judgment seat of Christ, when the Lord will open the Book of Life and not find their names written in it (Revelation 20:11–15). They will be cast out of His presence for all eternity. Christians will not face this terrible day of judgment, because our names are already permanently written in God's Book of Life. Yet the Lord will still examine our lives, giving and withholding rewards according to our level of obedience to His Word.

It is important for Christians to keep these things in mind as we go through our lives, remembering always that the Lord will one day hold us accountable for how we live. As Paul reminds us, "each one's work will become clear; for the Day will declare it, because it will be revealed by fire; and the fire will test each one's work, of what sort it is. If anyone's work which he has built on it endures, he will receive a reward. If anyone's work is burned, he will suffer loss; but he himself will be saved, yet so as through fire" (1 Corinthians 3:13–15).

↜ Digging Deeper ↝

5. What did Solomon mean when he said that "the righteous and the wise and their works are in the hand of God" (Ecclesiastes 9:1)? What are the implications of this truth?

6. What does it mean to "fear God and keep His commandments"? How is this done?

7. *What part did the day of judgment play in Solomon's thinking? What part does it play in your own priorities?*

8. *Have you ever gone through a time when you hated life? What caused your despair? What brought you out of it?*

ᕽ Taking It Personally ᕽ

9. *Where is your treasure? Is your focus on eternity, or on the here and now?*

10. *Are you prepared for the day of judgment? Is your name written in God's Book of Life? If not, what is preventing you from asking God to write it there now?*

∿ HISTORICAL BACKGROUND ∿

Solomon was renowned as the wisest man who ever lived, and people traveled great distances to learn from him. During his lifetime, he spoke three thousand proverbs and wrote more than one thousand songs (1 Kings 4:30–34). We will focus on the book of Proverbs for most of the remaining studies, since it is a vast storehouse of wisdom.

A proverb is a short, pithy saying that expresses a general principle of life, often giving advice on how to live wisely. Modern American examples include "An apple a day keeps the doctor away," "A penny saved is a penny earned," and others that are frequently repeated in conversation. The book of Proverbs is a collection of wise sayings that teach us, in very practical terms, how to gain understanding and live with wisdom. The vast majority of these proverbs were written by Solomon himself, but there were also other authors of certain sections. Solomon may have compiled this collection during the later years of his life.

Most of the book of Proverbs consists of succinct observations about life, many of which teach wisdom by contrasting opposites, such as the wise man versus the fool, or the diligent person versus the sluggard. Solomon began the book, however, with insights into the value of wisdom itself. He warned his reader that there was some work involved in attaining true wisdom, but the rewards to be gained are more precious than gold.

∿ READING PROVERBS 2:1–22 ∿

SEEK, SEARCH, CRY OUT: *The process of gaining wisdom requires deliberate effort on our part.*

1. MY SON: Much of the book of Proverbs uses the motif of a wise father instructing his son in the ways of wisdom. It is also possible that some passages reflect teachings that David passed on to Solomon in his youth.

RECEIVE . . . TREASURE: Three steps are necessary if a person is to become wise. First, he must be willing to receive or hear instruction from another who is wiser, and second he must value wisdom as more precious than great treasure. The third step, as we will see in this and future studies, is to act on those wise teachings. It is not enough merely to listen and learn; one must also obey if he is to become wise.

2. INCLINE YOUR EAR TO WISDOM . . . APPLY YOUR HEART: This phrase reiterates the steps toward wisdom from verse 1: one must first listen, then actively apply.

WISDOM . . . UNDERSTANDING: *Wisdom* means "skill," and refers to the quality that enables a person to live life skillfully, avoiding the world's countless traps and pitfalls. *Understanding* refers to one's mind, specifically the intellectual discipline required to gain wisdom. God calls His people to work toward a deep understanding of His Word, and to apply that Word in our lives. These things lead to wisdom.

3. CRY OUT: This suggests that one must desire wisdom to attain it—desiring it to the point of crying out to find it. Yet it also reminds us that all true wisdom comes only from God, and all we need to do is ask Him to give it to us (James 1:5–8).

4. SEEK . . . SEARCH: The process of acquiring wisdom is twofold: we are to ask the Lord, and we are to "seek" or "search." Part of the seeking step is an act of faith, as James tells us: "If any of you lacks wisdom, let him ask of God, who gives to all liberally and without reproach, and it will be given to him. But let him ask in faith, with no doubting, for he who doubts is like a wave of the sea driven and tossed by the wind" (James 1:5–6). The seeking or searching also encompass obedience, for true wisdom is very practical, requiring us to obey what we understand from God's Word.

SOME BENEFITS OF WISDOM: *Wisdom and understanding bring many benefits to those who possess them.*

5. THE FEAR OF THE LORD: This phrase refers to a reverent respect for God and obedience to His commands. Knowledge of God comes through a close, personal relationship with Him, available to everyone through His Son Jesus.

7. THE UPRIGHT: Those who are upright have been redeemed by the blood of Christ and continue to walk in obedience to His Word. Only the upright can hope to find the wisdom of God.

9. RIGHTEOUSNESS AND JUSTICE, EQUITY: True righteousness can only come through the sacrificial death and resurrection of Jesus Christ; it is a gift that is freely bestowed upon all who believe in Christ, and cannot be earned by anyone's good works. On a different level, however, righteousness can refer to acts of obedience to God's Word, as it does here. Justice is a quality of God's character, and those who behave justly are acting in a godly manner. Equity refers to fairness and impartiality, the quality of treating all people on an equal level. This, too, is a trait of God's character, who is no respecter of persons (Romans 2:11).

10. WHEN WISDOM ENTERS YOUR HEART: Wisdom is not mere head knowledge; it is a practical, daily lifestyle, a living out of the principles of God's Word. It must enter one's heart in the sense that practical obedience must become a constant habit if one is to become wise.

11. DISCRETION: This is the quality of being able to discern what course of action is right and fitting. It is similar to prudence, another quality that is found in the book of Proverbs.

12. THE MAN WHO SPEAKS PERVERSE THINGS: The world is full of those who preach false doctrine, urging us to depart from obedience to God's Word. Wisdom enables a person to recognize such false teachings and to avoid those who speak perversely.

16. THE IMMORAL WOMAN: The book of Proverbs refers to the immoral woman repeatedly, and we will consider these teachings in a later study. The principles can be applied just as easily to a wayward man, however, as any form of sexual immorality leads only to destruction.

17. FORGETS THE COVENANT OF HER GOD: This refers to the marriage covenant, a sacred vow made in the presence of God. Any sexual behavior apart from marriage is forbidden in Scripture.

⤳ READING PROVERBS 4:1–27 ⤳

IN ALL YOUR GETTING: *Life is filled with obligations and demands, but Christians must always keep wisdom as our top priority.*

2. GOOD DOCTRINE: The Word of God is the source of all true wisdom. Any counsel that goes against God's Word is not genuine wisdom.

3. I WAS MY FATHER'S SON: Solomon's parents were David and Bathsheba, and it is quite likely that many of the proverbs contained in this book were things that David had told Solomon. God commanded His people to train their children in His laws (Deuteronomy 6:7), and that principle still applies today: parents should be diligent to train their children in godly wisdom.

5. DO NOT FORGET: Wisdom is not something that one acquires once and for all; being wise requires daily refreshing from the Word of God. It is too easy to forget true wisdom when we allow our lives to become cluttered with the things of this world. Those who wish to become wise must constantly be immersing themselves in Scripture and godly teaching.

7. IN ALL YOUR GETTING: Life is filled with "getting": one must get a paycheck, get an education, get groceries, and on and on. It is very easy to become obsessed with getting, however, as we accumulate possessions and strive to advance in career or social circles. Solomon warned his readers that they must be constantly on guard to keep getting wisdom and understanding as their first priority.

8. WHEN YOU EMBRACE HER: This metaphor implies deep intimacy, suggestive of the marital embrace between a man and wife. The wise man has a deep love for God's ways, and he takes His Word into the most intimate parts of his life.

12. YOUR STEPS WILL NOT BE HINDERED: People during Solomon's day wore long, flowing garments that could easily become entangled in one's feet while walking or running. To guard against this, people would hitch up their robes and secure them under their belts. The image here suggests that life's concerns and temptations can also trip us up, but wisdom will help us make safe paths for our feet.

13. TAKE FIRM HOLD OF INSTRUCTION: Notice the imperatives in this verse: take firm hold; do not let go; keep. If we consider the true value of wisdom, of more worth than gold or gems, we will be determined to hang on to it at all costs.

THE ENEMY OF OUR SOULS: *We must not lose sight of the fact that the devil and the world system are constantly warring against God's people.*

14. THE PATH OF THE WICKED: The book of Proverbs frequently presents the reader with two choices: the way of evil and the way of wisdom. The world teaches us that life is complicated, that most decisions are various shades of gray, that there are many paths from which to choose, and so forth; but God's Word teaches us that there are only two ways to choose from: the wicked ways of the world, and the wise ways of God. Anything that does not adhere to the teachings of Scripture is part of the path of the wicked.

16. UNLESS THEY MAKE SOMEONE FALL: Life is not merely a passive series of choices; we have an enemy who actively seeks our destruction. The devil uses countless tactics and devices to lead men and women away from God, and he is always at work against us. Those who do not actively follow the paths of righteousness inevitably follow the path of wickedness, and they end up doing the devil's work.

19. THEY DO NOT KNOW WHAT MAKES THEM STUMBLE: This can be seen in the world around us, as people pursue ungodliness and then are puzzled at the inevitable results.

23. KEEP YOUR HEART: That is, guard your mind. Whatever we take into our minds will influence our speech and behavior; therefore, it is vital that Christians steep their minds in Scripture.

ᐁ FIRST IMPRESSIONS ᐁ

1. What are some of the rewards and benefits of wisdom, according to Proverbs 2 and 4?

2. Define each of the following, and give practical examples.
Wisdom:

Understanding:

Justice:

Equity:

3. *Why does Solomon warn us not to forget wisdom? How does one forget? What causes this to happen? How can it be avoided?*

4. *What does it mean to "embrace" wisdom? How is this done? Why is it important?*

⌁ Some Key Principles ⌁

Gaining wisdom requires deliberate effort.

Great athletes understand that it takes hard work to excel in their sport. Wealthy people will acknowledge readily that money does not grow on trees but requires diligence and shrewdness to attain. Practically any field of endeavor necessitates hard work if one is to advance—and wisdom is no exception.

This is balanced, of course, with the fact that God gives wisdom as a free gift to those who ask (James 1:5–8), for He is the source of all true wisdom, and no one can become wise apart from Him. Yet wisdom and understanding also require diligent effort on our part: the effort of obedience to God's Word and diligence in studying His Word. We must put God's Word into practice if we want to gain wisdom.

Nevertheless, it is well worth the effort, for wisdom pays large dividends. There are the temporary rewards of honor and longevity mentioned in Proverbs, but the real benefit of wisdom is eternal: the more one lives in wisdom, the more he becomes like Christ. Nothing else on earth is of more value than that.

Life presents a choice: wisdom or folly.

Life in this fallen world offers countless paths that lead away from God and toward destruction, but in reality there are only two different paths: the path of wisdom or the path of folly. While the world has all manner of counsel and advice, everything it offers is in fact on the same path—it all leads to destruction. .

So-called "wisdom" that is from the world is easier to obtain and easier to follow than the wisdom that comes from God. For this reason, the path of the world is wide, and it seems like everyone is on it. But the path of wisdom is narrow, and there are few who find it. Consider how Jesus described it: "Wide is the gate and broad is the way that leads to destruction, and there are many who go in by it" (Matthew 7:13). This is contrasted with the path of wisdom: "Narrow is the gate and difficult is the way which leads to life, and there are few who find it" (v. 14).

Fortunately, we are not alone! God gives His Spirit to Christians to indwell us and teach us the wisdom from above, enabling us to live with skill and become more like Christ. He is the Counselor, the one who shows us all things that are true and who enables us to follow the path of wisdom.

Parents should deliberately teach their children in the ways of wisdom.

Wisdom does not come naturally to children—quite the contrary, in fact. Proverbs tells us that "foolishness is bound up in the heart of a child" (22:15), reminding us that all humans are born sinners and foolish behavior comes naturally to us all. This same verse, however, teaches us to replace a child's folly with wisdom by using "the rod of correction."

The "rod of correction" includes far more than corporal punishment, however. David imparted wisdom to Solomon by teaching him from God's law. He also modeled wisdom for his son, demonstrating by his own lifestyle what it meant to be a man after God's own heart. This did not mean that David was perfect; the Bible records some grievous sins in his life, including, as mentioned previously, his early relations with Bathsheba, who came to be Solomon's mother.

No Christian parent is perfect; we all wrestle with our own sin, and so we all make bad decisions from time to time. Yet David's success in teaching wisdom to his son demonstrates that God uses sinners to teach other sinners His ways. This is especially true of parents and their children, and God's Word makes it clear that parents have a responsibility to train up their children in the ways of wisdom. "And these words which I command you today shall be in your heart. You shall teach them diligently to your children, and shall talk of them when you sit in your house, when you walk by the way, when you lie down, and when you rise up" (Deuteronomy 6:6–7).

✍ DIGGING DEEPER ✍

5. Why did Solomon place such stress on searching and crying out for wisdom? What part do our efforts play in gaining wisdom? What part does God play?

6. What is the "path of the wicked"? What is the "path of righteousness"? How does one discern between the two?

7. What does it mean to "keep your heart with all diligence" (Proverbs 4:23)? How is this done? Why is it important?

8. What tactics does the world use to lead people away from wisdom? What tactics does Satan use? Give practical examples.

9. How well are you teaching wisdom to others in your life, such as your children? Which speaks louder: your words or your actions?

10. How much do you value wisdom in your own life? What things compete most insistently for your attentions and efforts?

SECTION 2:

CHARACTERS

In This Section:

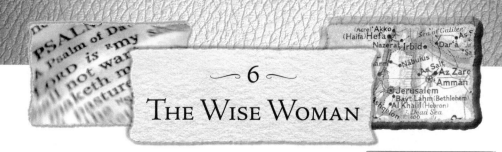

～ 6 ～
THE WISE WOMAN

～ CHARACTER'S BACKGROUND ～

The first few chapters of Proverbs focus on a father's admonition to his son to avoid immorality, so it is fitting that the last chapter be a mother's advice to her son about what a godly woman should look like. Thus it appeals to both men and women. To sons, it is a description of the woman to marry. For daughters, this is a description of the woman to emulate. While the book of Proverbs as a whole describes the life of wisdom, this last chapter describes a wife of wisdom. It describes a married woman who appears to have some financial resources at her disposal, yet the principles outlined are widely applicable.

The woman of wisdom may seem intimidating at first. She rises before dawn and works until well after sunset, and her efforts are all focused on serving others. She is very capable in the domestic arts of creating clothing and gourmet meals, but she is equally competent in commerce, demonstrating shrewdness in financial affairs and even running a small business. Very few people possess all the qualities of the Proverbs 31 woman, but all Christians can strive to imitate her example.

The chief quality of the woman of wisdom is that she serves others with a willing heart—and this is an aspect of wisdom that all God's people can acquire with the help of the Holy Spirit.

～ READING PROVERBS 31:1–31 ～

A MOTHER'S WARNINGS: *Chapter 31 opens with one "King Lemuel" remembering his mother's wise words of advice.*

1. KING LEMUEL: Nothing is known of any King Lemuel. Ancient Jewish tradition identifies him with Solomon himself, who—perhaps because of his own sexual immorality—may have been using a pseudonym in this chapter to pass on the wise teachings of his mother, Bathsheba. *Lemuel* means "belonging to God."

HIS MOTHER TAUGHT HIM: The book of Proverbs places heavy emphasis on the importance of a father's teachings, but men do not have a monopoly on wisdom—or on the responsibility for teaching it to one's children.

3. Do not give your strength to women: It was common for ancient kings to have many wives. We have already seen how Solomon did this very thing—and suffered greatly for it. He could attest from firsthand experience that such behavior "destroys kings." Yet the principle applies equally to all people, young and old: sexual promiscuity is self-destructive.

5. forget the law: Drunkenness can lead a person to disregard the teachings of God's Word, even to the point of engaging in sinful behavior that one might not even consider while sober. Alcohol can pervert one's judgment and moral standards, which is all the more dangerous for anyone who holds a position of authority.

6. Give strong drink to him who is perishing: Such extreme situations, possibly relating to a criminal on death row or someone agonizing in pain with a terminal illness or tragic circumstance, are in utter contrast to that of the king.

8. Open your mouth for the speechless: Christians are called to defend those who cannot defend themselves, just as God defends His children.

A Virtuous Wife: *We are now introduced to a remarkable woman, a wife and mother who runs her household with skill.*

10. a virtuous wife: Verses 10–31 form an acrostic poem, each verse beginning with the next letter of the Hebrew alphabet. The "virtuous wife" in this verse refers to a woman who is noble, morally upright, and faithful to her husband. For single men, this becomes a description of the woman to marry. For women, this is the description of the woman to be.

11. her husband safely trusts her: The wise woman is faithful to her marriage vows, and she is also prudent with the family's finances. Her husband's complete trust in her brings the family "no lack of gain."

13. wool and flax: Wool and flax were used to make clothing and linen. The Hebrew for *seek* means "to search for diligently." The wise woman takes extra pains to find the things her family needs, considering both good quality and reasonable cost.

willingly works with her hands: The wise woman is also willing to make things for her family, not relying on the workmanship of others. The book of Proverbs sets high value on diligence and labor, contrasting them with the indolence of the sluggard.

15. rises while it is yet night: The wise woman is selfless in serving her household, starting her day early on behalf of others.

a portion for her maidservants: She is also generous with those who help her, even with those outside of her immediate family. Notice also that there is no hint of a grudging attitude in her selfless service.

16. She considers a field and buys it: Women in the ancient world were not typically involved in business transactions, yet the wise woman transcended cultural expectations in service to her family. The Hebrew word for *consider* implies careful thought and advance planning. She is not shopping for shopping's sake; rather, she has her eyes set on the future. She is not an impulse shopper, but she gives thorough consideration to her finances and searches out the most profitable purchases for her family's long-term benefit.

she plants a vineyard: The wise woman also reinvests the money she saves by purchasing sensibly, and her motivation is always for the good of the family, not for selfish gain.

17. She girds herself with strength: That is, she does her work vigorously and with zeal. It is a simple truism that you accomplish more when you work with effort. Thus, the wise woman is contrasted with the sluggard.

A Successful Businesswoman: *The wise woman is not held hostage by the world's expectations. She finds work to do that increases her family's comfort.*

---

18. her merchandise is good: The wise woman takes pride in all the labors of her hands, striving toward excellence in all she does. There is no sense that she considers any labor too menial or that she expects the praises of others for all her hard work. She regards excellence for her family as enough reward in itself.

her lamp does not go out by night: The woman who rises before daylight also stays up well after sunset in service to her household.

19. distaff . . . spindle: These were parts of the loom, used for spinning thread and making garments. She is taking responsibility for the clothing and appearance of her family.

20. She extends her hand to the poor: The wise woman pours herself out in service to her family—and also finds time to reach out to the poor outside her household. The verbs "extends" and "reaches out" emphasize that this is a deliberate effort, not an afterthought. She can afford to be concerned for others because she has already made provision for her own. The emphasis on "her household" in these verses, however, suggests that her family's needs come first.

21. She is not afraid of snow: The wise woman plans ahead for her family's needs, meeting those needs in advance. When the snow falls, her husband and children are already warmly clothed. Note that she is not afraid of snow *for her household*, rather than for herself, emphasizing her selfless motivation.

22. tapestry for herself: This is the first time that the wise woman has done anything for herself—and even here it benefits the entire household with rich furnishings.

FINE LINEN AND PURPLE: Purple and scarlet (v. 21) required expensive dyes and were usually worn only by royalty. The wise woman has used her own efforts to gather and create the very best for her family, clothing them like kings.

A SUPPORTIVE WIFE: *The wise woman also encourages her husband in his work and ministry, and he excels because of her support.*

23. HER HUSBAND IS KNOWN IN THE GATES: To sit in the city gates indicated a position of wisdom and influence. The wise woman advances her husband's career by her vast support behind the scenes.

25. STRENGTH AND HONOR ARE HER CLOTHING: It is striking that all other mention of clothing in these verses has referred to the wise woman's family, not to herself. Her own clothing is far more valuable, as she is adorned with strength and honor. For the wise woman, inward beauty is more important than outward adornment.

IN TIME TO COME: The wise woman does not strive for immediate gain, but always has her eyes focused on the future. This, in fact, is one of the keys to her success, as she has placed her treasure in eternity rather than in temporal advancement.

26. OPENS HER MOUTH WITH WISDOM: The book of Proverbs addresses the power of speech a great deal, as we will see in Study 7. The wise woman's speech is always seasoned with grace and kindness (see Colossians 4:6).

28. HER CHILDREN RISE UP: The wise woman has also taken care to teach her children to walk in wisdom. When they grow into godly adults, they remember her example and call her blessed.

30. CHARM IS DECEITFUL AND BEAUTY IS PASSING: Contrast this with the teachings of the world today, which put such emphasis on a woman's outward appearance. Over time, youthful beauty fades. But for the godly woman, time only increases the invaluable beauty of her character.

ᔕ FIRST IMPRESSIONS ᔕ

1. *What does verse 3 mean by the command "Do not give your strength to women"? How does sexual promiscuity destroy one's strength? How does this command apply to women?*

2. *What does it mean to "open your mouth for the speechless" (v. 8)? How is this done? Who are the speechless?*

3. *How does the wise woman benefit her household?*

4. *List below some qualities of the "virtuous wife," defining them in your own words. How is each acquired? How do they apply to an unmarried woman? To a man?*

↜ Some Key Principles ↝

The wise woman serves others rather than herself.

The world urges us to serve ourselves first and foremost. The modern "self-esteem" movement teaches that we must learn to love ourselves before we can love others. This, however, is a form of wisdom from below, the type of false wisdom that leads us away from godliness.

The wise woman, by contrast, is always looking for ways to serve others. She puts her family first, striving to meet their immediate needs and also looking ahead to the needs of the future. When she has finished with those priorities, she turns her attention to the needs of her neighbors, reaching out generously to the poor and afflicted. In all these things, the wise woman does not see herself as a martyr but as doing for others what God has done for her.

The wise woman of Proverbs 31 used her resources to help others, rather than to satisfy her own desires and needs. In so doing, she served the Lord cheerfully and reaped an abundant reward. Today, Galatians 5 reminds us, "For you, brethren, have been called to liberty; only do not use liberty as an opportunity for the flesh, but through love serve one another. For all the law is fulfilled in one word, even in this: 'You shall love your neighbor as yourself'" (v. 13–14).

The wise woman is prudent.

Prudence is the skill of exercising sound judgment in practical matters. The prudent person takes time to consider what course of action will be best in a given situation, rather than acting without thought. Another word for prudent is *circumspect*, from the Latin word meaning "to look around," or in other words, to see an issue or circumstance from all sides. Prudence makes a person discerning, capable of seeing the truth of a matter when others might not.

The woman of Proverbs 31 demonstrated prudence with her family's finances. She carefully considered the potential strengths and weaknesses of a field before purchasing it (v. 6), examining what the investment would bring and what it would cost. She was prudent in planning ahead for the winter months, making warm clothes for others before they were needed. She was prudent in her speech, sharing gentle wisdom with others in due season, and speaking on behalf of those who could not defend themselves.

Wisdom and prudence are always seen together, as Solomon wrote in an earlier proverb: "I, wisdom, dwell with prudence, and find out knowledge and discretion" (8:12). We grow in wisdom when we take time to prayerfully consider things from God's perspective. Such wisdom is not acquired quickly, as prudence requires us to carefully deliberate before acting or speaking. This is contrary to our human nature; we often find ourselves wanting to react to circumstances immediately and with passion. But the course of wisdom consists in prudence, taking the time to ask for wisdom from God and learning to see the world through His eyes, rather than our own.

The wise woman radiates an inner beauty.

Modern society places great emphasis on external appearances. We are bombarded with images of physical beauty from all realms of entertainment, while the advertising industry insists that we must spend our money and time making ourselves look good according to constantly changing worldly standards of beauty. Our culture stresses physical exercise and diet, while ignoring those pursuits that produce spiritual strength and character.

It is interesting that the Bible tells us nothing about Jesus' physical appearance. In fact, Isaiah suggests that He was a rather plain and ordinary-looking man: "He has no form or comeliness; and when we see Him, there is no beauty that we should desire Him" (Isaiah 53:2). When God became a man, the world despised Him and rejected Him. Rather than being "a god among men," who drew men to Himself with His radiant appearance, He became "a Man of sorrows and acquainted with grief. And we hid, as it were, our faces from Him; He was despised, and we did not esteem Him" (Isaiah 53:3).

God is not concerned with our physical appearance but with our spiritual character. The woman of Proverbs 31 understood this and focused her energies on cultivating godliness and virtue. Ironically, her inner beauty radiated outward, giving her a brilliant countenance that could not have been imitated with cosmetics. She was clothed with strength and honor (v. 25), and she was praised more than those who possessed great charm and physical beauty (v. 30). God is pleased when we pursue such inner beauty, calling us to exercise ourselves toward godliness. "For bodily exercise profits a little, but godliness is profitable for all things, having promise of the life that now is and of that which is to come" (1 Timothy 4:8).

∽ Digging Deeper ∾

5. *What does it mean to be girded with strength? How is this accomplished? What are its results?*

6. *Why did the Proverbs 31 woman extend her hand to the poor? What role does such giving play in gaining wisdom?*

7. What does it mean, in practical terms, to be prudent? Give examples of prudence from your own life or people you know.

8. In what ways does the Proverbs 31 woman go against today's culture? How do the world's teachings compare with her priorities?

⌐ TAKING IT PERSONALLY ⌐

9. Is your focus on perfecting outward appearances, or on developing inner beauty? What inner qualities might the Lord be calling you to improve?

10. Which qualities of the Proverbs 31 woman do you see in yourself? In what areas do you fall short of her high standards?

~ 7 ~
THE WISE SPEAKER

↳ CHARACTER'S BACKGROUND ↰

"Talk is cheap," the old saying goes, implying that words are not as important as actions. In some instances this can be true, yet it belies an important fact that Scripture emphasizes: our words do matter. Jesus confirmed this when He commanded His disciples, "Let your 'Yes' be 'Yes,' and your 'No,' 'No'" (Matthew 5:37). And James warned his readers that "the tongue is a fire, a world of iniquity" (James 3:6). Our words have tremendous power—both for good and for evil.

We worship a God who created the universe by the power of his word. When God speaks, everything in the universe obeys. Moreover, Jesus Himself *is* the Word (John 1:1). One of the ways people are distinguished from the lower orders of creation is by the power of speech; we were given language as a gift from God, and He expects His children to use that gift to glorify the One who gave it.

The book of Proverbs is filled with admonitions on how to use speech correctly, along with warnings concerning those who use their words for evil. Proverbs tells us that the wise person will be one whose words are filled with knowledge and understanding. The fool, by contrast, has no understanding, because he has cut himself off from the source of all knowledge: the God who created him.

In this study, we will learn what it means to use our gift of language wisely, and we will also discover that wise speech can help a person grow in wisdom.

↳ READING PROVERBS 10:10–14, 18–21, 31–32 ↰

SPEAKING IN LOVE: *The wise person will speak the truth at all times, but his words will be tempered with love.*

10. HE WHO WINKS WITH THE EYE: That is, one who hints and makes insinuations, while not openly making any accusations that can be verified or refuted. Such communication can destroy another person's reputation without any risk to the accuser.

A PRATING FOOL: One who chatters incessantly.

11. A WELL OF LIFE: The wise man's speech leads others toward righteousness and eternal life by encouraging them to godliness and reminding them of the Gospel.

12. LOVE COVERS ALL SINS: The hateful person spreads abroad ill reports of his enemies, which "stirs up strife." The wise person, in contrast, does not repeat such gossip, thus covering another person's transgressions with love. Peter quoted this verse in 1 Peter 4:8.

13. HIM WHO HAS UNDERSTANDING: Notice the connection between understanding and wisdom. The person who speaks with wisdom is first circumspect, considering a matter before commenting on it. Understanding comes from a diligent study of God's Word, while wisdom comes from consistent obedience to that Word. The two operate together to give one wise speech.

DEVOID OF UNDERSTANDING: The fool, by contrast, does not consider his ways; neither does he examine his life in light of God's Word. His speech is therefore mere empty prattle. He might consider himself wise, but the rod of correction awaits him.

14. WISE PEOPLE STORE UP KNOWLEDGE: This storehouse is filled from the study of Scripture. As one's storehouse of knowledge grows, it will overflow into wise words.

THE MOUTH OF THE FOOLISH IS NEAR DESTRUCTION: The wise man is reticent, determined to think carefully before answering, but the fool is quick to respond while also devoid of wisdom. His words will bring about his own destruction.

⤳ READING PROVERBS 15:1–7, 23, 28 ⤶

SPEAKING WITH KNOWLEDGE: *The wise person's speech will also be filled with knowledge, drawn from the storehouse of Scripture.*

1. A SOFT ANSWER: We can use words both to build up and tear down. A gentle answer, which comes from a heart of love, can stop a war before it even begins.

A HARSH WORD STIRS UP ANGER: A soft answer can defuse anger that exists, but harsh words can actually create anger where none existed before.

2. USES KNOWLEDGE RIGHTLY: It is important to notice that there is a right way and a wrong way to use knowledge. God gives us knowledge, understanding, and wisdom so that we may become more like Christ, and to help others become more like Him too. The right way to use knowledge, therefore, is to apply it to oneself first and then gently help others move toward godliness. It is wrong to use knowledge for self-aggrandizement or for browbeating others. The temptation to use knowledge wrongly is perhaps why Paul said that "knowledge puffs up, but love edifies" (1 Corinthians 8:1).

4. A WHOLESOME TONGUE: The wholesome tongue speaks words that nurture and bring healing. Its speech is nutritious, not poisonous.

TREE OF LIFE: The tree of life was planted in the garden of Eden (Genesis 2), and it will flourish again in the New Jerusalem (Revelation 22). You may recall that it was created to bring eternal life to the eater. It is sobering to realize that today God uses our *words* to lead people toward eternal life. But when we speak as fools, we bring perverseness into our conversation, just as the serpent did when he lied to Eve and led her astray. Our words can either lead people toward Christ or away from Him; Proverbs makes no mention of any neutral ground.

7. DISPERSE KNOWLEDGE: The wise person's speech will be seasoned with his knowledge of God's character and His Word. Yet this proverb should also be balanced by verse 2, above.

⌇ READING JAMES 3:1–12 ⌇

SPEAKING LIKE WILDFIRE: *James warns us that our tongues are an unruly evil, set on fire by the flames of hell. The wise person will strive for mastery of the tongue.*

1. TEACHERS: This word refers to those who preach and teach in an official capacity, such as pastors of local churches. Nevertheless, the principle applies to any Christian who teaches others about godliness, including parents who instruct their children. When you teach, you are expected to live according to the same doctrines that you instruct others to follow. God is the One who holds people accountable to this higher standard. Wise speech brings with it a responsibility to live in obedience to God's Word.

2. WE ALL STUMBLE: That is, we make mistakes continually. This refers to sinful behavior, anything that offends the holiness of God.

STUMBLE IN WORD: Speech may be the easiest area in which to fall short of God's glory. It is human nature to speak glibly and without much thought, yet that is precisely the time when we are most apt to say inappropriate things.

A PERFECT MAN: In Bible times, the word *perfect* often meant "mature." The mature believer will have control over the tongue, using words to encourage others toward godliness. Conversely, this also suggests how hard it is to keep one's tongue under strict control. No one is perfect, and everyone says things, at least now and then, that are not godly.

BRIDLE THE WHOLE BODY: The person who gains mastery over his own tongue will also be strong enough in godliness to control his whole body. James was suggesting that the tongue is the weakest member of our bodies, yet the most unruly. Therefore, it should be a primary focus of our efforts toward godliness.

3. BITS IN HORSES' MOUTHS: The horse is a powerful beast, yet it is brought completely under the rider's domination by controlling its tongue. This image suggests that whatever force controls one's tongue will control the whole man—whether that is the sinful nature or the Holy Spirit.

4. DRIVEN BY FIERCE WINDS: A person's tongue can be driven by fierce passions, just as a ship is driven by winds. Yet this also suggests that the tongue can be controlled by the Holy Spirit, who will guide it toward godliness at all times.

WHEREVER THE PILOT DESIRES: James used both ships and horses to demonstrate how the entire body is guided by the tongue. Our words can lead to actions, both our own and others'. When our speech is guided by the Holy Spirit, we are piloted by God Himself.

6. THE TONGUE IS A FIRE: Fire spreads rapidly, destroying everything in its path. Words can have the same effect; consider how fast gossip spreads, and what destructive effect it can have on the lives of others. Fire can also burn the one who wields it, in the same way that our own words can damage our lives.

IT IS SET ON FIRE BY HELL: God used the Word to create the universe, but Satan perverted the power of words when he seduced Eve to eat the forbidden fruit. The evil one continues to use words today to lead people away from God, and Christians must be constantly on guard against the dangerous force of the tongue.

8. NO MAN CAN TAME THE TONGUE: This would be bad news for us if the story ended here. What good would James' admonitions do concerning the tongue if we were powerless to control it? But Christians have the Holy Spirit living within, and it is through His power that one tames the tongue.

9. WE CURSE MEN: James emphasized throughout his letter that Christians must treat other people with gentleness and respect, for to do otherwise is hypocrisy. Mankind was created in the image of God (Genesis 1:26–27), so everyone we meet bears God's imprint (similitude). How can we bless God with one breath, but then curse those who bear His image with the next? God calls us to be consistent with our speech—consistently godly.

ᔕ FIRST IMPRESSIONS ᔕ

1. *What kind of speaker "winks with the eye" (Proverbs 10:10)? What does this mean? How can a person detect such motives?*

2. *Where does understanding come from? What does it refer to? Why is it important in one's speech?*

3. *How is knowledge different from understanding? Where does it come from? Why is it important to correct understanding?*

4. *When have you seen someone use knowledge rightly? Use it wrongly? What constitutes right use of knowledge versus wrong use?*

❧ Some Key Principles ❧

Our words affect our actions and the actions of others.

Life seems to be filled with talk. The media bombards us with words; politicians prate ceaselessly about the economy and social affairs; people debate their opinions about everything under the sun. "It's all just words," we'll say, implying that words without action have no meaning.

But the Scriptures teach us that our words have a powerful effect, both on ourselves and on others. James used the illustration of a wildfire to indicate the destruction that can be caused by idle or careless speech. It can burn the person who utters it and scald the person who hears it. It can also spread its destruction in a wide circle, as one person's words are repeated by another. Each speaker's utterances lead to actions by himself or those around him.

This principle can also work in a positive way, however. As we learn to speak words of wisdom, we increase the likelihood that we will act in wisdom, and we encourage others to live in godliness. Consider James's analogy of a ship under the power of the wind: the pilot guides the rudder, and the rudder steers the whole ship. When we submit to the guidance of the Holy Spirit, He guides us in the use of our tongues, and our tongues can steer our lives into Christlike character.

Speak the truth in love.

The world teaches us that we should speak our minds freely, without regard to the effects our words may have upon others. Indeed, according to the world's wisdom, a person can become "repressed" or "inhibited" if he tries to bottle up his thoughts and passions. Therefore, say the experts, it is healthy to be a "straight shooter," to give free vent to every opinion—even (and usually) negative opinions and criticism.

Yet this is not how God wants His children to use their tongues. The book of James exhorts us to "be swift to hear, slow to speak, slow to wrath; for the wrath of man does not produce the righteousness of God" (1:19–20). God's Word repeatedly commands us to speak the truth—but to do so in a gentle and loving spirit (Ephesians 4:15). As Proverbs makes clear, lies and deception should never be found on the tongues of God's people; all our speech should be seasoned with knowledge and gentleness.

No one wants to be lied to, and no one enjoys harsh criticism—even if the criticism is true. We strengthen the body of Christ when we speak the truth in love. "Therefore, putting away lying, 'Let each one of you speak truth with his neighbor,' for we are members of one another. . . . Let no corrupt word proceed out of your mouth, but what is good for necessary edification, that it may impart grace to the hearers" (Ephesians 4:25, 29).

Wise speech grows from the storehouse of Scripture.

One of the things that distinguish the wise speaker from the fool is that he or she "uses knowledge rightly, but the mouth of fools pours forth foolishness" (Proverbs 15:2). The reason for this is simple: the fool *has* no knowledge of the things of God. Indeed, "the fool has said in his heart, 'There *is* no God'" (Psalm 14:1, emphasis added).

We do well to remember, however, that we are all fools by nature. As Proverbs declares, "foolishness is bound up in the heart of a child" (Proverbs 22:15). It is in the nature of all people to turn away from God and pursue folly, and it is only through the Holy Spirit and the Word of God that anyone can hope to gain knowledge and understanding.

Those who wish to grow in wisdom must store up knowledge, in much the same way that one stores grain in a warehouse or puts money in the bank. Our storehouse is built upon Scripture, and deposits are made through personal and corporate study of God's Word. Wise behavior grows out of wise words, and wise words grow out of one's knowledge of God's character. The more we study Scripture, the more our conversation will be seasoned with knowledge and understanding.

⌒ Digging Deeper ⌒

5. *What does it mean when we say that "love covers all sins" (Proverbs 10:12)? When have you experienced this? How is this balanced with speaking the truth?*

6. *When have you seen a soft answer turn away wrath? When have you seen inflammatory speech stir up wrath? How does one gain the skill of defusing anger?*

7. What did James mean when he said that the tongue "is set on fire by hell" (James 3:6)? When have you experienced this yourself? What is the cure?

8. If no man can tame the tongue (James 3:8), then what hope is there of gaining control over it? What role does God play in this? What role do you play?

ᕦ Taking It Personally ᕤ

9. What influence do your words generally have in the lives of others? In your own life? How can the Holy Spirit help you improve in this area?

10. How well stocked is your storehouse of knowledge? How can you increase its contents?

~ 8 ~
THE FOOLISH SLUGGARD

PROVERBS 6, 12, 21, 26; 2 THESSALONIANS 3

↳ HISTORICAL BACKGROUND ↰

The book of Proverbs addresses many areas of fleshly behavior, both warning against the dangers and admonishing the reader to instead pursue godliness and wisdom. Solomon and the others who contributed to this book used caricatures, small word portraits of people who are controlled by carnal desires, to caution against living life according to the flesh.

One such caricature is that of the *sluggard*, a lazy person who indulges his fleshly desire for rest and pleasure. The sluggard does not like to work; he prefers to sleep long hours and eat gourmet meals. When he does work, he performs only the barest minimum needed to attain his more immediate goal: more rest and relaxation. Ironically, the sluggard simultaneously expends great creative energy in his pursuit of leisure time, dreaming up the most outlandish excuses to avoid work.

The principles we will consider in this study are aimed at the sin of sloth, but they apply just as well to any area of fleshly excess. The Lord wants His children to mortify the flesh, putting to death the passions that lead to destruction and cultivating the fruit of the Spirit. For the sluggard, this means throwing off the bedclothes and getting busy with the work that God has provided.

↳ READING PROVERBS 6:6–11 ↰

GO TO THE ANT: *The authors of Proverbs frequently consider the lower orders of creation to help us understand spiritual principles. One such creature is the lowly ant.*

6. GO TO THE ANT: The book of Proverbs repeatedly looks at the natural world for inspiration on wisdom. The ant provides a picture of industry and self-motivation, a stark contrast to a sluggard. The sluggard is a lazy person with no self-control, who uses his energies and resources to find excuses to avoid work.

7. NO CAPTAIN, OVERSEER OR RULER: The ant does not need to be commanded to work; neither does it have to be supervised to ensure that it carries out its responsibilities correctly. In these verses, the contrast with the sluggard is implied; while the ant needs no supervisor, the sluggard must be driven to work by someone else.

8. PROVIDES HER SUPPLIES IN THE SUMMER: The ant looks ahead to the future, laying up stores when work is easy to provide for times when work is scarce. Summer and harvest refer to those times when work is plentiful and appropriate, anticipating the scarcity of winter, when food will not be available. Such cycles are natural in life, but the sluggard does not look ahead or make provisions for the future.

9. SLUMBER . . . SLEEP: The sluggard is characterized in Proverbs as one who loves to sleep. There is nothing inherently wrong with rest and relaxation; rest is, after all, another facet of life's natural cycles. But the sluggard overindulges in sedentary activities. In modern parlance, one might call him a couch potato.

10. A LITTLE SLEEP: The sluggard has a habit of excusing his slothfulness "just this once," and asking for "just a little more." We can all relate to the temptation, when the alarm goes off in the dark hours, to indulge in just a few more minutes in bed. The sluggard's life is characterized by such thinking.

11. LIKE A PROWLER . . . LIKE AN ARMED MAN: Proverbs constantly emphasizes the fact that laziness leads to poverty. The picture here is that poverty will overpower the sluggard, taking him captive and robbing him like an armed thief. When an armed robber kicks in one's door, it is too late to take precautions against him. Likewise, when the sluggard realizes that he is impoverished, it will be too late to do anything about it.

⌒ READING PROVERBS 12:11, 24, 27 ⌒

THE DILIGENT SHALL RULE: *Laziness leads to enslavement, but the person who works with diligence will rise to roles of leadership, and the sluggard will end up working for him.*

11. HE WHO TILLS HIS LAND: The diligent man pursues whatever labor he finds to do—if he owns land, he cultivates it and uses it for his own profit. The principle is not dependent upon ownership of land, but rather describes an attitude toward the work that one has at hand. The hardworking person does his job faithfully, regardless of what that job might be.

HE WHO FOLLOWS FRIVOLITY: The sluggard, by contrast, is not interested in doing his work; he "lives for the weekend," and his focus is always on the pursuit of pleasure and entertainment. Such people are always on the lookout for get-rich-quick schemes.

24. The hand of the diligent will rule: Those who are self-motivated and industrious invariably rise to positions of authority over those who are not.

the lazy man will be put to forced labor: The ant was pictured earlier as a creature that requires no overseer, but the sluggard will not work unless he is driven by others. The lazy man needs an overseer, who is pictured here as a slave driver.

27. what he took in hunting: It is interesting that the sluggard is shown here as actually working, making the effort to go out hunting for his food. But the implication is that he was probably forced to it, as in verse 24 above. Once the overseer's whip is removed, the sluggard reverts to his natural ways, too indolent even to roast his own food. He might actually work sometimes, but he rarely finishes what he starts.

diligence is man's precious possession: That is, it is a precious treasure, which a person should strive to attain.

⤳ Reading Proverbs 21:5, 17, 25–26 ⤳

Get-Rick-Quick Schemes: *The sluggard desires wealth as much as anyone—he just doesn't want to work for it. His conflicting desires will destroy him.*

5. everyone who is hasty: The contrast here is between the diligent, who carefully plan ahead, and the sluggard, who hopes to get rich quickly and with little investment. The diligent worker makes a concerted effort at every step of a project, striving to do his best and produce quality work. The sluggard, on the other hand, maintains a "good enough" work ethic.

17. He who loves pleasure: When the sluggard does work, his motivation is to attain pleasure. The diligent, by contrast, work with a long-term perspective. Wine and oil suggest luxury and self-indulgence, things the diligent avoid but the sluggard craves.

25. The desire of the lazy man kills him: The sluggard often has very expensive tastes, and he covets the lifestyle of the rich and famous. The problem is that he is unwilling to expend long-term effort in acquiring the resources to live in high style— even if such a goal were worthwhile. (Proverbs makes it abundantly clear that such a goal leads a man to destruction.)

26. the righteous gives and does not spare: The wise person is not focused on such temporal riches and luxuries, but on eternal treasure. This focus enables the wise to give to the poor, rather than consuming one's wealth on dissipation and pleasure.

↗ Reading Proverbs 26:13–16 ↖

The Rusty Hinge: *The lazy man expends a great deal of energy finding excuses to avoid working. His problem is that he is wise in his own eyes.*

13. There is a lion in the road: The book of Proverbs frequently makes fun of the sluggard, using humor to underscore the extent to which a lazy person will go to avoid work—even to inventing ludicrous excuses. The effort involved in avoiding work is scarcely less than what would be required to get up and do it!

14. As a door turns on its hinges: Here is another humorous portrait of the sluggard. One can picture him swinging from side to side, as securely attached to his bed as a door is to its frame.

15. buries his hand in the bowl: The sluggard is often made weaker by wealth. This man had food in his bowl, making it unnecessary (for the moment) to get up and find something to eat. Yet even in this good fortune, he was too lazy to feed himself what he had.

16. wiser in his own eyes: To be wise in one's own eyes is a grave danger, according to Proverbs: "Do you see a man wise in his own eyes? There is more hope for a fool than for him" (26:12). The solution to this danger is to recognize that there is no true wisdom apart from God. "Do not be wise in your own eyes; fear the Lord and depart from evil. It will be health to your flesh, and strength to your bones" (Proverbs 3:7–8).

↗ Reading 2 Thessalonians 3:10–15 ↖

Avoid the Sluggard: *Paul takes a strong stand against the sin of sloth, warning that those who don't work shouldn't eat. He calls Christians to hold one another accountable.*

10. If anyone will not work: Paul wrote this epistle to the Christians in Thessalonica to address a number of specific issues, one of which evidently was that some believers there were not working for a living. Much of the letter concerns the return of Christ, and it is possible that some believers were using hope for the rapture as an excuse to avoid work. Note that Paul spoke of those who *won't* work, as opposed to those who *can't* work for some legitimate reason.

neither shall he eat: Paul's basic premise is simple: if you want to eat, you'll have to work. This principle does not preclude Christian charity; rather, it counterbalances it.

Christians are commanded to share their blessings with others, but those who receive are also commanded to be diligent in whatever work the Lord has made available to them.

II. A DISORDERLY MANNER: The Greek word translated "disorderly" was used to describe soldiers who had stepped out of rank in marching formation. Those who refuse to work for a living are refusing to follow the prescribed rule, declining to fulfill their own natural obligations.

BUSYBODIES: The sluggard has too much time on his hands, and he fills it with destructive pursuits. Those who have no affairs of their own to attend to inevitably begin to meddle in the affairs of others.

12. WORK IN QUIETNESS: It is an interesting paradox that when the sluggard does find work to do, he generally makes a big show of being busy. The cure for gossip and interference is to be busy with one's own work.

EAT THEIR OWN BREAD: Paul commanded the Thessalonians not to live on handouts and charity, but to meet their own basic needs.

13. DO NOT GROW WEARY IN DOING GOOD: This is the most important work for God's people: to be diligent in doing good. This involves first meeting one's own obligations, then sharing the Lord's blessings with others.

14. DO NOT KEEP COMPANY WITH HIM: Christians are commanded not to be socially involved with sluggards. This withdrawal of companionship was intended to force the idle man to meet his own needs, rather than relying on the pity of others. The goal was "that he may be ashamed" and therefore repent of his disobedience to God's commands.

16. ADMONISH HIM AS A BROTHER: This withdrawal of companionship was not intended to be a punishment but an admonishment. *Admonish* means literally "to advise toward," or in other words, to counsel, warn, or remind a person of his duties. The goal was to remind those who refused to work that they had an obligation to do so. They were not enemies of the Christians, merely brothers who needed some correction. Paul was directing the Thessalonians to hate the sin but love the sinner.

⌁ FIRST IMPRESSIONS ⌁

1. *In what ways does an ant differ from a lazy person? What other creatures demonstrate diligence and industry?*

2.   What motivates a person to be lazy? What motivates a person to be diligent and industrious? How can you cultivate diligence and avoid sloth?

3.   What does it mean to "follow frivolity" (Proverbs 12:11)? Give specific examples. What is the opposite of this behavior?

4.   What does it mean to be hasty? How is this also consistent with being lazy? What motivates a person to be this way?

ᐧ Some Key Principles ᐧ

Christians should work for a living.

The sluggard hasn't got the energy to do any work, although, ironically, he does have the energy to contrive outlandish excuses to avoid it. He also tends to enjoy the finer things in life, appreciating luxury and fine dining—preferably at someone else's expense. Any work that he does perform is done halfheartedly, with the expectation of a generous paycheck while not concerning himself in the least with the quality of his work.

God's people should not live this way. As we saw earlier, the satisfaction that comes from working hard is one of the gifts of grace that God gives men (see Ecclesiastes 2:24). God made men for a task, and when a man works hard at that task, he not only provides for his family, but he brings glory to God.

Paul laid out the principle in simple terms: he who does not work does not eat. This does not provide an excuse for Christians to turn a blind eye to people who are in need. It does, however, demand accountability from those who refuse to work, even when they have ability and opportunity. Meeting one's basic needs is a Christian's duty.

The love of money is a sin.

The sluggard may work hard to avoid work, but when he's got work, he doesn't like to work hard at doing it. Wealth is always appealing, but the effort required to gain it is not. Consequently, the sluggard is easily susceptible to the sin of loving money.

Paul writes that "the love of money is a root of all kinds of evil" (1 Timothy 6:10). This is because it causes people to become more obsessed with the things of this world and less passionate about the things of God. When someone loves money, they become stingy and they close their hand to the poor. They make decisions based on finances rather than on God's will. They forget that the riches this world offers are of no value in eternity. This is why Jesus said, "You cannot serve both God and money" (Luke 16:13, NIV).

This principle applies also to the daily work that the Lord has provided for each of us. A job is a gift from the Lord, and it is also a ministry that He expects us to perform to the best of our abilities—working as unto Him, not our earthly masters (Ephesians 6:5–8). As Solomon reminds us, "Whatever your hand finds to do, do it with your might; for there is no work or device or knowledge or wisdom in the grave where you are going" (Ecclesiastes 9:10).

Laziness leads to personal destruction.

The sluggard has an excessive love for rest and relaxation. These things in themselves are not sinful; the sin comes when leisure pursuits become a consuming passion. The person who sleeps or plays when he should be working will be overtaken by poverty, which will come upon him unexpectedly and irresistibly like an armed robber. The individual with too much time on his hands will also find things to do with that time that cause harm to him and to others, such as becoming a busybody who meddles in affairs that are none of his business.

This principle, of course, is not limited to laziness; it holds true for any fleshly passion that we allow to rule our lives. The sin of laziness is just one of many ways that Christians can permit their flesh to govern their lives, and the result is always crippling.

Paul confessed, "I know that in me [that is, in my flesh] nothing good dwells; for to will is present with me, but how to perform what is good I do not find . . . O wretched man that I am! Who will deliver me from this body of death?" (Romans 7:18, 24). The answer to this question is Jesus Christ—it is He who delivers us from the body of sin and from the eternal destruction which would otherwise be our fate. Thanks to Him, we have the power and presence of the Holy Spirit working in our lives, and He gives us the ability to subdue the flesh and obey His Word. And we *need* that. The ways of the flesh lead to destruction, but the ways of God lead to wisdom and eternal life.

⤳ Digging Deeper ⤳

5. *What does it mean to be wise in one's own eyes? How does a person become this way? Why is it dangerous? What is the antidote?*

6. Why did Paul decree that anyone who does not work should not eat? How do we balance this with the Lord's commands to care for the needy?

7. In what ways is a sluggard disorderly? What does this mean, in practical terms? What is required of Christians if we are to be orderly?

8. What does it mean to admonish another Christian? How is this done? When is it required? How does one balance this with not being a meddler or busybody?

9. How diligent are you in doing the work the Lord has given you? In your job? Your ministries? Your family life?

10. Is there an area of fleshly passion that is struggling for control in your life? How can you gain victory through God's Word? Through the power of the Holy Spirit?

∼ 9 ∼
THE SEXUAL FOOL

∼ CHARACTER'S BACKGROUND ∼

God created sex as a precious gift to His creation. It was meant to be a form of tenderness shared solely between a husband and wife, and God intended for men and women to refrain from that intimacy until He had blessed them with a mate. But sin has perverted God's original plan, and the world has polluted and twisted His delicate gift into all forms of aberrant sexual behavior. Nevertheless, God still calls His children to adhere to His original plan, making chastity a high priority in their lives.

Chastity refers to sexual purity, whether one is married or single. A married man is chaste when he confines his sexual intimacy to his wife, while a single man is chaste when he abstains completely from sexual activity. God's people are called to place a very high value on sexual purity, because sin in this area has a unique power to destroy a person's life.

This is not the world's perspective. Our culture today urges us to satisfy every lust, as though we were merely scratching an itch. Sexual promiscuity is healthy, we are told, while chastity is unhealthy. It is all part of natural human behavior, and we shouldn't make such a big deal about it.

But the book of Proverbs paints a very different picture. The fornicator is shown to be a fool, and the results of his sin lead to his inevitable destruction. The wise person will keep himself pure from sexual immorality.

∼ READING PROVERBS 5:1–23 ∼

LIPS OF KNOWLEDGE—OR HONEY: *Solomon opens his teachings by reminding us that our speech influences our behavior—and he contrasts it with the speech of an adulteress.*

1. MY SON: This chapter, like most of Proverbs, is written as instruction from a father to his youthful son. The principles of wisdom it contains, however, can apply equally well to men and women of any age.

LEND YOUR EAR TO MY UNDERSTANDING: Once again, we see that one gains wisdom only by being willing to learn and applying oneself to hearing wise instruction.

2. PRESERVE DISCRETION: *Discretion* comes from a Latin word meaning "separation." It implies the ability to separate right from wrong, to distinguish wisdom from folly. The person who has discretion is able to discern the wise course of action in any given situation.

YOUR LIPS MAY KEEP KNOWLEDGE: We saw in a previous study that the wise person will speak prudent words. Here we are reminded that wise speech is a skill that can be lost. By avoiding sexual sin, a person will be able to retain knowledge in his speech.

3. THE LIPS OF AN IMMORAL WOMAN DRIP HONEY: In contrast to the wise person, the immoral woman's speech is dripping with honey. Honey is sweet—cloyingly sweet—but it lacks substance, as opposed to the speech of wisdom, which is substantially endowed with knowledge. Solomon pointed out elsewhere, though, that such sweet speech has a place—within the proper bounds of marriage (see Song of Solomon 4:11).

HER MOUTH IS SMOOTHER THAN OIL: In other words, her words are slick with flattery and lies.

4. BITTER AS WORMWOOD, SHARP AS A TWO-EDGED SWORD: Wormwood is a bitter plant that grows in desolate areas. It symbolizes the bitterness and desolation that inevitably result from sexual promiscuity. The adulteress's seduction began sweet and smooth, but it ended in bitterness, violence, and death.

FEET THAT RUSH TO DESTRUCTION: *The adulteress's feet lead her away from her home and out into the streets. The feet of the fool lead him to the grave.*

5. HER FEET GO DOWN TO DEATH: The book of Proverbs speaks frequently about one's feet, which represent the direction in which one is walking. The sexual fool sets his feet in motion when he pursues immorality, but his footsteps are ultimately leading him to death and destruction.

6. HER WAYS ARE UNSTABLE: That is, she is shifty and inconsistent, making her ways incomprehensible to the one whom she seduces. The sense also suggests that she is unstable specifically to avoid thinking about her inevitable destination. She deliberately avoids considering her ways, not wanting to face the pit that lies before her.

7. DO NOT DEPART FROM THE WORDS OF MY MOUTH: Again we are reminded that the wise must continually choose to walk in wisdom. Solomon's own life demonstrated that a wise man can depart from wisdom.

8. REMOVE YOUR WAY FAR FROM HER: Compare Joseph, who literally fled from the temptations of a seductress, leaving his cloak in her hands (see Genesis 39:1–12).

DO NOT GO NEAR THE DOOR OF HER HOUSE: Some temptations are unavoidable, but there are things we can do to protect ourselves. The person who wants to avoid sexual immorality can begin by avoiding the situations that cater to it.

9. LEST YOU GIVE YOUR HONOR TO OTHERS: Sexual depravity can cost a young person his honor and reputation—if not worse.

10. LEST ALIENS BE FILLED WITH YOUR WEALTH: The sexual fool also gives away something of inestimable value—his chastity—to complete strangers, thus robbing both himself and his future wife.

11. WHEN YOUR FLESH AND YOUR BODY ARE CONSUMED: This can certainly apply to venereal diseases, a risk that is all the more deadly in this age of HIV and AIDS. Yet it also conveys the sense of dissipation that accompanies sexual immorality.

12. HOW I HAVE HATED INSTRUCTION: The passions of youth gradually fade with age, and growing old gives one a chance to look back at the decisions he or she has made. The sexual fool will spend his latter days wallowing in regret, remembering the times that he was warned against his folly and ruing the fact that he didn't listen.

PURE WATERS OF REFRESHMENT: *Solomon likens godly intimacy with cool waters in a dusty desert. Those waters should be protected, for they bring health.*

15. DRINK WATER FROM YOUR OWN CISTERN: That is, enjoy the intimate pleasures of your own spouse. Such intimacy can be as refreshing and healthful as cool water in the arid desert—when it is undertaken within the confines of marriage. Solomon wrote much about the joys of wedlock in Song of Solomon, but in Proverbs he addressed those who indulged their fleshly appetites contrary to God's commands.

16. SHOULD YOUR FOUNTAINS BE DISPERSED ABROAD?: Water in the Middle East was a valuable commodity, not to be wasted by pouring it out in the streets. Similarly, the sexual fool gives his precious gift of intimacy wantonly, sharing a valuable treasure with strangers.

21. HE PONDERS ALL HIS PATHS: This is a sobering reminder that the eyes of God are always fixed upon His children. This is a tremendous blessing, because it demonstrates how deeply He loves us and how intimately involved He is in our lives. Yet His attentiveness to our actions also means that He observes the things that we attempt to do in secret.

22. HE IS CAUGHT IN THE CORDS OF HIS SIN: Sexual immorality is a deadly trap, and it is difficult to extricate oneself once one is entangled. The image is that of a man caught in a net or webbing; the more he struggles to get free, the more ensnared he becomes. And the net is of his own making.

↜ Reading Proverbs 7:1–27 ↝

Guard Your Eyes: *The Word of God is a source of life and wisdom, and God's people should make it an intimate part of their lives.*

2. the apple of your eye: That is, one's pupil. We instinctively protect our eyes because sight is so essential. In the same way, the wise person will diligently protect his soul by carefully walking in obedience to God's Word.

3. Bind them on your fingers: This is similar to tying a string around one's finger as a reminder to do something. Christians should take pains to always remember that obedience to God is paramount. One's wedding ring might also serve as a literal, visual reminder of the importance of sexual purity.

Write them on the tablet of your heart: Memorizing Scripture is an invaluable tool in avoiding all manner of temptation, and it also increases one's storehouse of knowledge, leading to greater depths of wisdom.

7. the simple: To be simple in the parlance of Proverbs has nothing to do with one's intellectual abilities, but rather with one's moral weakness. The simpleton of Proverbs is a fool, a person who has willfully rejected instruction.

The Fool Heads to Destruction: *Solomon looks out of his window and notices a young man wandering in the streets. He watches as the fool heads to his own downfall.*

7. A young man devoid of understanding: Understanding comes from knowledge, and knowledge comes from listening to instruction. The young man described here lacks understanding through his own fault, because he has disregarded wise teaching.

8. he took the path to her house: This story graphically illustrates the warnings of Proverbs 5:8, which we considered earlier in this study. The young man deliberately set his steps toward the house of the adulteress, rather than avoiding her door, and here we see the results of this foolishness.

9. In the black and dark night: This brings to mind John 3:19, which says, "Men loved darkness rather than light, because their deeds were evil." We deceive ourselves when we think that we can keep our sins hidden, even in the black of night, yet this is just how the sexual fool deludes himself.

10. a crafty heart: The word translated *crafty* literally means "to guard, keep secret." The woman had been watching for him, waiting as a spider in its web, and she took great pains to hide her true intentions from the foolish youth.

The Prowling Seductress: *As the young fool looks for pleasure, a dangerous foe looks for a victim. That foe is the adulterous woman.*

11. LOUD AND REBELLIOUS: Folly is personified in Proverbs as a loud woman (9:13), implying that folly is constantly clamoring for our attention. The adulteress is always drawing attention to herself in the hopes of seducing a fool. She is also rebellious, departing willfully from the ways of God—which is equally true of this foolish young man.

HER FEET WOULD NOT STAY AT HOME: The adulteress also rejected the notion that a wife should be a homemaker. Instead, she wandered idly through the streets, looking for victims to destroy. In this, she is like the devil, who "walks about like a roaring lion, seeking whom he may devour" (1 Peter 5:8).

12. LURKING AT EVERY CORNER: The sexual fool is like a beast of prey, prowling and lying in wait for victims. This again underscores the similarity to Satan.

13. WITH AN IMPUDENT FACE: The sexual fool boldly insists that her folly is not wrong; she is insolent and aggressive. "This is the way of an adulterous woman: She eats and wipes her mouth, and says, 'I have done no wickedness'" (Proverbs 30:20).

14. TODAY I HAVE PAID MY VOWS: The adulteress went beyond claiming innocence in her actions to the point of actual self-righteousness. The world today does the same thing by insisting that a person has a perfect right to do whatever he desires with his body. One is almost performing an act of righteousness in committing sexual immorality, according to this thinking.

18. DELIGHT OURSELVES WITH LOVE: The sexual fool mistakes physical intimacy with love. Love is a self-sacrificing commitment to another person's welfare, and sexual intimacy should be an expression and outgrowth of that commitment within marriage. But the fool removes the sexual act from that context and makes it mere self-gratification.

22. AS AN OX GOES TO THE SLAUGHTER: The images used to describe the youthful fool all underscore the bestial aspect of sexual sin. The ox is a dumb brute, incapable of understanding what is about to happen to it. The bird is noted for its low intelligence and it is easily caught in the snare. The "fool to the correction of the stocks" can also be translated as "a stag stepping into a snare," which is immediately shot through with the hunter's arrow. All these beasts can be excused for not recognizing their danger, but the sexual fool is without excuse.

26. ALL WHO WERE SLAIN BY HER WERE STRONG MEN: The fool thinks that he will be the exception to every rule, the one who will commit folly unscathed. But sexual wickedness destroys even those who are strong, and there are no exceptions.

∽ FIRST IMPRESSIONS ∽

1. *What does it mean that the adulteress's lips drip with honey? What does this image suggest about sexual temptation? How is this different from the wise man's speech?*

2. *In what sense do the feet of the sexual fool "go down to death" (Proverbs 5:5)? How does sexual immorality lead to death?*

3. *In what sense is the sexual fool unstable? How are the ways of the wise person stable? How is this stability acquired?*

4. *In what way does the sexual fool give his honor to others? How does sexual purity guard against this?*

⤳ Some Key Principles ⤳

Sexual immorality leads inevitably to death and destruction.

The world teaches us that sex is merely a pleasurable leisure activity, as natural and inconsequential as a handshake. Advertising, the news media, people we meet in daily contact, and all forms of popular entertainment take it for granted that sex apart from marriage is normal and healthy, to the point that it is an unspoken assumption that individuals who are attracted to each other should consummate their relationship as soon as possible.

But God's Word makes it abundantly clear that sex was intended by our Creator to be an act of intimacy shared only by two people—a man and a woman—within the bonds of marriage. Anything other than this is a perversion of what God intended, and any deviation from His created order leads only to dire consequences. Proverbs does not overstate the case when it makes clear that sexual immorality leads to death and destruction. The collapse of the nuclear family in modern Western society proves this to be true.

God's people are commanded to remain pure from sexual sins. This includes adultery as well as fornication, sexual intimacy between people who are not married to one another. Paul exhorts us in very strong terms on this matter: "But fornication . . . , let it not even be named among you, as is fitting for saints; . . . For this you know, that no fornicator . . . has any inheritance in the kingdom of Christ and God. Let no one deceive you with empty words, for because of these things the wrath of God comes upon the sons of disobedience. Therefore do not be partakers with them" (Ephesians 5:3, 5–7).

Do not simply resist sexual temptation—flee from it.

Sexual passion is a powerful force, and when used correctly it can help to solidify the bond between a husband and wife. But used improperly, it will lead to destruction, as we have already seen. The temptation toward sexual sin can be so alluring that a wise person will do more than simply resist it—he will run away from any potential threat of temptation before the evil one even has a chance to tempt him.

Joseph provided us with a good example of this tactic. He was a slave in the household of a powerful Egyptian named Potiphar and was entrusted with all that his master owned. Potiphar's wife came to him and commanded him to lie with her, and she persisted in that demand day after day. Finally, she took hold of Joseph in an attempt to drag him off to temptation, but the young man turned and fled from her presence. (See Genesis 39 for the whole story.)

We all face some temptations that simply require endurance and repeated determination to resist, but there are other temptations that can best be avoided by running as fast as possible. Paul advised Timothy, "Flee also youthful lusts" (2 Timothy 2:22). In other words, the only escape from this temptation is to run the other way.

The wise person protects his purity as a precious treasure.

Our culture scorns the concept of chastity. Those who remain virgins until marriage are considered odd misfits, old-fashioned fuddy-duddies, even deviants of sorts. In the eyes of the world, promiscuous sex is considered healthy, a normal part of growing up, an inherent right of every individual, and as sacred as though it were guaranteed by the Constitution.

But God's Word teaches us that sexual purity is a precious treasure, something we should guard as carefully as we guard our eyesight. Solomon makes it clear that the wise person fights against the lusts of the flesh, while the fool gives into sexual immorality. Because healthy sexual intimacy is found *only* within the parameters of marriage, in that setting it is a great blessing to God's people.

It is obvious that sexual sin has a unique power to destroy a person's life. It is the sin that brought David down, as he slept with Solomon's own mother, Bathsheba. It was the sin that first attacked the early church (see 1 Corinthians 5:19; Acts 15:20), and it is perhaps the most prevalent sin in our culture today. Paul taught us that sexual sin is so unique, that when we sin sexually, we sin against the Holy Spirit Himself. "Flee sexual immorality," wrote Paul. "Every sin that a man does is outside the body, but he who commits sexual immorality sins against his own body. Or do you not know that your body is the temple of the Holy Spirit who is in you, whom you have from God, and you are not your own? For you were bought at a price; therefore glorify God in your body and in your spirit, which are God's" (1 Corinthians 6:18–20).

ᠵ Digging Deeper ᠵ

5. Why did Solomon use the image of cisterns of water to describe sexual intimacy within marriage? What does this suggest about the proper use of God's sexual gifts?

6. How did the young man in Proverbs 7 get involved with the prostitute? Trace his steps, looking for the things that he did to get there. How might he have avoided the problem?

7. Why did Solomon compare the sexual fool to an ox? A bird? What do these comparisons suggest about sexual sin?

8. Why is it that sexual sin can be so destructive in a person's life?

↬ TAKING IT PERSONALLY ↫

9. Do you guard your purity as carefully as you guard your eyesight? Are there areas of impurity in your life that the Holy Spirit would have you clean out?

10. Why is it best to flee from some temptations, rather than stand firm and resist? How does one flee from sexual temptations?

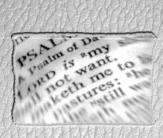

SECTION 3:

THEMES

IN THIS SECTION:

STARTING STRONG, FINISHING STRONG

PROVERBS 1, 3; HEBREWS 12

~ THEMATIC BACKGROUND ~

Solomon was the wisest man who ever lived, yet he did not finish his life well. Something happened along the way that caused him to stop walking in wisdom and to resort instead to walking according to the flesh. If the wisest man of all time did not finish strong, how can an ordinary Christian hope to do any better?

The truth is that wisdom is not a onetime acquisition; it is a lifestyle, a daily commitment to walk according to the Word of God. Solomon did not finish strong because he neglected the Word of God, and when someone strays from God's Word, he will inevitably stray from wisdom. Finishing strong requires daily *application* of God's Word to our lives. Since biblical wisdom is practical, it is seen in daily decisions and in a person's lifestyle. It is not merely a collection of knowledge.

If the Christian life is a race, then finishing strong is key. When someone becomes a Christian, he is not miraculously transported to heaven but is left on earth to fight the fight of faith and to run the race that is laid out before him. Endurance is achieved when a person submits his life to the teachings that are in God's Word and then seeks to apply those teachings through the power of the Holy Spirit. When we submit to the Spirit, He will show us the areas in which we need to strengthen our walk and purify our lives—and He will give us the power to do it.

This process involves more discipline than a normal race, but the stakes are much greater. But when we rely on the Spirit of God to help us fight sin and grow in grace, we will be enabled to finish the race—and finish strong.

~ READING PROVERBS 1:20–33 ~

WISDOM CALLS OUT TO THE SIMPLE: *Wisdom is personified as a woman, standing in the public square and calling out to the passersby.*

20. WISDOM CALLS ALOUD OUTSIDE: Wisdom is personified as a woman in this passage. She calls aloud in the public square, suggesting that knowledge of God and wisdom to live according to His principles are readily available to anyone who seeks them. Wisdom is not restricted to those with education or a good background or any other attribute; it is a free gift of God, given to any who request it (James 1:5).

22. YOU SIMPLE ONES: The "simple ones" are those who have not given much thought to wisdom. They are naive but not as far gone in folly as the outright fool. Proverbs makes it clear that there is little hope for the fool to change his wicked ways, but the simple may yet consider their ways and become wise.

SCORNERS: A scorner is a person who openly mocks the things of God. He has heard the words of wisdom but has rejected them.

FOOLS HATE KNOWLEDGE: The fool does not realize that he hates knowledge; many fools, in fact, are very learned people. But the person who hears the Word of God and rejects it has treated it with contempt, and he therefore hates wisdom.

23. TURN AT MY REBUKE: To turn is to repent, to recognize that one is heading in the wrong direction and rotate 180 degrees to go the opposite way. Proverbs places great importance on the ability to accept a rebuke; it is one of the things that distinguish the wise man from the fool. The wise person will hear a judicious rebuke, examine his ways to see where he has strayed from God's path, and turn back to the right way.

I WILL POUR OUT MY SPIRIT ON YOU: True wisdom comes from God alone, and He is eager to pour it forth through His Spirit into our lives. But to receive that outpouring, we must first obey what He has revealed to us. Wisdom grows only through practical application as we obey God's Word.

24. I HAVE CALLED . . . I HAVE STRETCHED OUT MY HAND: Notice that wisdom is the one who always takes the initiative, reaching out to those who need her. It is God who makes the overtures to humanity, offering us salvation and wisdom as free gifts—but it is up to us to accept those gifts.

THE FATE OF THOSE WHO REFUSE: *Wisdom warns her hearers that there are dire consequences for ignoring her free offer.*

25. WOULD HAVE NONE OF MY REBUKE: David sinned against God when he committed adultery and murder, but he repented when he was rebuked (2 Samuel 12). Solomon had been commanded by God not to marry foreign women, but he disregarded that command. David's willingness to accept a rebuke enabled him to finish his life well, being called "a man after God's own heart" (Acts 13:22). In contrast, Solomon did not heed the

Lord's rebuke, but continued obstinately in his sinful ways—and he did not finish the race as he had begun.

26. I ALSO WILL LAUGH AT YOUR CALAMITY: The universe declares the glory of God, and every person has a conscience that convicts of sin and points to the truth of the gospel. Yet people go to great lengths to reject those warnings, and they spend their lives taking good things from God (such as rain, food, family, pleasure) without thanks, all the while speaking wickedly of God and refusing to submit to him. When the day of judgment comes, sinners who have rejected wisdom may call on God for relief, but their cries will be met with derision.

28. BUT I WILL NOT ANSWER: It is important to understand that the day of grace does not last forever. God offers wisdom and salvation in this life, but the time will come when salvation is no longer offered, and instead judgment will be levied.

29. THEY HATED KNOWLEDGE: A person who rejects the knowledge of God demonstrates hatred for knowledge—even though he may think he is a knowledgeable person who enjoys learning. The only knowledge that counts for eternity is knowledge of God.

30. DESPISED MY EVERY REBUKE: God's rebukes are vital because they are designed to keep us close to Him and walking in the paths of wisdom and righteousness. They are not the harsh punishments of a slave master, but the gentle reproofs of a teacher who wants His pupil to excel. The person who finishes well will listen carefully to the rebukes of wisdom.

31. THEY SHALL EAT THE FRUIT OF THEIR OWN WAY: The Bible makes it clear that we reap what we sow (Galatians 6:7). The fool insists upon sowing seeds of folly, so he will inevitably eat its fruits.

32. THE COMPLACENCY OF FOOLS WILL DESTROY THEM: Complacency is a deadly sin, as it numbs a person to the promptings of the Holy Spirit. The spiritual life of a Christian is compared to running a race, as we will see shortly, but the complacent Christian is like a runner who gains ground in a race, only to sit down in the shade and take a nap. We must keep moving forward, following the Word of God through the leadership of the Holy Spirit, if we want to finish the race admirably.

33. WHOEVER LISTENS TO ME WILL DWELL SAFELY: The good news in this is that God does not abandon His children, leaving us to finish the race in our own power. He is constantly at work to keep us on the right path, strengthening our character and faith to become more like Christ. Anyone who listens to the teachings of God will run the race effectively.

ᨑ READING PROVERBS 3:1–35 ᨑ

REMEMBER GOD'S LAW: *Wisdom does not guarantee that a man will finish the race well. Solomon's life demonstrates this. We must take care not to forget God's Word.*

1. DO NOT FORGET MY LAW: Here again we are reminded that we must make a diligent effort to put God's law into practice, studying it and meditating on it regularly. If we do not maintain our daily diet of God's Word, we run the danger of forgetting His law.

2. LENGTH OF DAYS AND LONG LIFE AND PEACE: These are among the temporal blessings that wisdom bestows. It is noteworthy that Solomon did not enjoy these benefits, finishing his days earlier than he might have otherwise, amid great turmoil in his kingdom. He began his race with great wisdom but gradually forgot God's law.

3. NECK . . . HEART: Wisdom is both internal and external. We incorporate it into our lives as we store up knowledge in our hearts through God's Word, then apply it outwardly in obedience. It becomes a beautiful adornment that money cannot buy. The outward manifestation of wisdom causes a wise person to find favor in the eyes of man, while God is pleased to look upon the wise person's heart.

5. WITH ALL YOUR HEART: Solomon's heart was led away from the Lord over the course of his life, in contrast to his father, David, who served the Lord with his whole heart throughout his lifetime. This does not mean that David never sinned, as we have already mentioned, but that he guarded his heart against allowing other priorities to compete with his devotion to God. The Lord said, "Judah has not turned to Me with her whole heart, but in pretense" (Jeremiah 3:10), suggesting that God's people can make an outward show of devotion to Him while still setting up idols in their hearts. If we want to finish the race well, we must allow the Lord to root out such pretenses, creating in us a whole heart devoted solely to Him (Jeremiah 24:7).

LEAN NOT ON YOUR OWN UNDERSTANDING: In other words, do not depend upon your earthly wisdom to understand what God is doing in your life. The word *lean* means "support yourself," suggesting that a person can depend upon his own fleshly perspective to find wisdom—but this leads only to sin and folly.

PRACTICAL WISDOM: *Solomon offers advice on how to put wisdom into daily practice. As we honor the Lord, He will guide our paths.*

IN ALL YOUR WAYS ACKNOWLEDGE HIM: That is, deliberately remind yourself that God is absolutely sovereign over all the affairs of your life, and He is in control of every circumstance. As we acknowledge His lordship in our daily lives, we will grow to serve Him in all things.

HE SHALL DIRECT YOUR PATHS: This can often include hardship and suffering, as well as prosperity and pleasure. But when we remember to acknowledge His sovereign hand, we will be able to trust that He is leading us down the best possible path.

7. DO NOT BE WISE IN YOUR OWN EYES: As we have seen in an earlier study, this is a grave danger. The person who is wise in his own eyes is depending upon fleshly wisdom, the wisdom from below, to deal with the circumstances of life. The humble person, by contrast, recognizes that all true wisdom comes from above, from God alone, and he asks faithfully for God to grant him wisdom.

FEAR THE LORD AND DEPART FROM EVIL: These two things go hand in hand. Fear of the Lord is a deep respect for His authority, which leads naturally to obedience to His commands. Wisdom is very practical; it must be put into practice to become true wisdom—it is not mere head knowledge.

9. HONOR THE LORD WITH YOUR POSSESSIONS: God's people should remember that everything we have is a gift from God, including all that we possess. He wants us to use His gifts in His service to others, not in selfish pursuits. This includes regular tithing, giving Him the "firstfruits" of all our increase, and not selfishly hoarding our possessions but generously using them in His service.

DO NOT DESPISE CORRECTION: *Wisdom is an active process, and there are times when we must all be chastised. The wise man does not fight against God's correction.*

11. DO NOT DESPISE THE CHASTENING OF THE LORD: Once again, we are reminded of the importance of the Lord's correction in our lives. The wise man accepts correction, remembering that he is sinful and imperfect, whereas the fool despises correction and remains wise in his own eyes.

12. WHOM THE LORD LOVES HE CORRECTS: God's hand of discipline is not cruel and arbitrary but is loving and gentle. His rebukes are always intended to help us grow stronger. He does not delight in pointing out our shortcomings; He delights in seeing us become more and more like Christ.

19. THE LORD BY WISDOM FOUNDED THE EARTH: The Bible tells us that Jesus was the agent of creation: "In the beginning was the Word, and the Word was with God, and the Word was God. He was in the beginning with God. All things were made through Him, and without Him nothing was made that was made" (John 1:1–3). Therefore, as we increase in wisdom, we become more like Christ, and we gain more wisdom by imitating Him continually.

21. LET THEM NOT DEPART FROM YOUR EYES: By keeping our eyes on Christ and imitating Him in all that we do and say, we will steadily attain the wisdom from above.

25. TROUBLE . . . WHEN IT COMES: Solomon acknowledged that everyone faces troubled times, even the wise, as we saw in Study 4. The wise man is distinguished from the fool in the way he responds to trouble when it comes. The fool races about in fear and panic, depending on his own earthly wisdom to deal with the crisis, while the wise man reminds himself that God is sovereign. He can be fully trusted in every circumstance.

27. DO NOT WITHHOLD GOOD: In verses 27–31, Solomon listed numerous examples of very practical wisdom. It is noteworthy that all have to do with our relationships with our neighbors. The truly wise man learns to love others as he loves himself, humbly considering others as better than himself (see Matthew 22:39 and Philippians 2:3).

32. THE PERVERSE PERSON: The perverse person does things his own way, disregarding the commands of God. The Lord withholds wisdom from those who refuse to obey Him, but He shares His inmost confidences with those who follow His commands.

35. SHAME SHALL BE THE LEGACY OF FOOLS: Only the wise will finish the race with excellence. Those who persist in going their own way will end their days as fools.

⌁ READING HEBREWS 12:1–11 ⌁

RUN THE CHRISTIAN RACE: *The author of Hebrews gives us some practical advice on how to finish strong. He likens the Christian's life to a race—a long and difficult pursuit.*

1. WE ARE SURROUNDED BY SO GREAT A CLOUD OF WITNESSES: This refers back to the many saints described in the previous chapter of Hebrews. It does not mean that the Old Testament saints are watching us like spectators at a race; rather, their lives provide examples and testimonies to help us understand how to run the race with diligence.

LAY ASIDE EVERY WEIGHT: An athlete who is running in a marathon works hard to make his clothing as lightweight as possible. No marathon runner would dream of wearing combat boots or of carrying a backpack filled with toys. In the same way, a Christian must be on guard at all times to prevent the things of life from becoming a burden—possessions, temporal pursuits, leisure activities, and so forth.

THE SIN WHICH SO EASILY ENSNARES US: Solomon provided an example of the dangers of ensnaring sin. He was the wisest man who ever lived, yet he did not finish the race well because his feet became ensnared. The image is of a marathon runner going cross-country, not running on a cultivated gravel track. There are countless things to trip on when running through the woods and countryside, and the athlete keeps an eye on the path in front of him to prevent himself from being tripped up. The same principle holds true for the believer: we must be constantly examining our path, watching for those sins and temptations that threaten to make us fall.

RUN WITH ENDURANCE: The Christian life is a marathon, not a short sprint. Wisdom requires daily maintenance, a regular diet of Scripture reading, prayer, and obedience. The Greek word translated "race" is the root of our English word *agony*. The implication is that endurance requires hard work, sometimes enduring difficult times of suffering and hardship. We must not give up on our walk with Christ if we intend to finish the race well.

2. THE AUTHOR AND FINISHER OF OUR FAITH: Jesus is the author of our faith because it is through Him that salvation is possible. As the author of our faith, one might say that He wrote the book of faith. He is the paramount example of what it means to walk in wisdom. He is also the finisher of our faith, because He is always working to complete in us the fullness of His image: "being confident of this very thing, that He who has begun a good work in you will complete it until the day of Jesus Christ" (Philippians 1:6). We do not run the race alone or under our own power.

FOR THE JOY THAT WAS SET BEFORE HIM: This seems incongruent: that Jesus looked at the cross with joy. This joy was not *in* the sufferings but it came *through* the sufferings, as Jesus was then able to make atonement for sin, once and for all.

3. LEST YOU BECOME WEARY AND DISCOURAGED IN YOUR SOULS: Discouragement and despair are the enemies of our souls. Christians must guard against such thinking, keeping in mind what Jesus endured for our sakes as He completed the work that the Father gave Him. Again, this involves keeping our eyes focused on the eternal rather than on the temporal.

11. NO CHASTENING SEEMS TO BE JOYFUL FOR THE PRESENT: Here is the core of finishing strong: the resolve to accept chastening as from God, recognizing that it is intended to strengthen our souls. If Solomon had heeded the Lord's words concerning foreign wives, he could have finished strong, yet he refused. David, on the other hand, did heed the Lord's rebuke, and he remained wholehearted for God to the end of his days.

∽ First Impressions ∾

1. Why is wisdom pictured standing in the public square, calling to passersby? What does this teach about wisdom? About human nature?

2. What role does chastisement play in gaining wisdom? In keeping wisdom? Why is it important?

3. Why does wisdom say that she will laugh at the calamity of those who reject her offer? Why is this a fitting response to mockers and scorners?

4.   *What does it mean to eat the fruit of one's own way (Proverbs 1:31)? What is the fruit of folly? What is the fruit of wisdom?*

↶ Some Key Principles ↷

We must take care not to forget God's Word.

Proverbs teaches us that knowledge of God's Word is essential if we are to gain wisdom. Yet it also reminds us that we can easily forget His Word, causing us to stray from the paths of wisdom into any number of foolish pursuits. This is precisely what happened to Solomon, despite his strong beginning. He had been granted immense wisdom in his young adulthood, yet he gradually forgot the very commands that the Lord had given him concerning pagan practices.

We run the danger of forgetting God's Word when we fail to obey and apply it. We increase our knowledge by spending time in private study of Scriptures and corporate times of worship and teaching. Beyond this, it is imperative that we remember that wisdom is very practical: it must be used if it is to flourish.

We use our wisdom when we obey God's commands. This in turn helps us see the world as God sees it, which is of course the ultimate measure of wisdom. But when a person understands God's Word but fails to obey it, he is like a man who looks into a mirror but forgets what he sees. The mirror ceases to be of any practical value, since we did not adjust our appearances from what we saw. The book of James reminds us, "Be doers of the word, and not hearers only, deceiving yourselves. For if anyone is a hearer of the word and not a doer, he is like a man observing his natural face in a mirror; for he observes himself, goes away, and immediately forgets what kind of man he was. But he who looks into the perfect law of liberty and continues in it, and is not a forgetful hearer but a doer of the work, this one will be blessed in what he does" (1:22–25).

The Lord uses rebuke and correction to keep us running the race.

Nobody likes to be criticized, and it can be very painful to be reprimanded. Even basic correction can be difficult to endure, especially when it is done in a harsh or demeaning manner. We've all encountered people who seem to delight in finding fault with others, and it is hard to see any value in such constant words of criticism.

Yet every athlete understands the importance of criticism. Criticism exposes weakness, which when corrected makes an athlete perform better. If an athlete ignores his coach, he is only hurting his own performance.

The same principle holds true in the Christian life. None of us is perfect, and we all fall short of the completed image of Christ. Like the athlete, we all have areas that need to be strengthened, and the sinful nature is constantly fighting to reassert itself—even in areas where we've gained victory in the past. That's why it is so important that we receive the Lord's corrections with a teachable spirit; as Jesus stated, "As many as I love, I rebuke and chasten. Therefore be zealous and repent" (Revelation 3:19).

We do not run the race alone or under our own power.

The world of athletic competition features some amazing accomplishments. Runners have set world records for speed; mountain climbers demonstrate incredible endurance; skydivers defy death by leaping from great heights—there are countless feats of prowess being undertaken by daring men and women all over the world every day. But there is one thing that all these feats have in common: they are within the realm of possibility for human endeavor.

That is not the case when it comes to the Christian race. We are called to be like Christ, but there is no person on earth who can accomplish that feat on his own power. We are all born under the curse of sin, and none of us can overcome that curse. Left to our own devices, no one could hope to live as Christ lived, for He was without sin. Thank God we are not left to our own devices!

God has given His Spirit to each believer—the very same Spirit that raised Christ from the dead (Romans 8:11)—and it is through His power and guidance that we overcome the sinful nature that holds us captive. Paul once cried, "O wretched man that I am! Who will deliver me from this body of death?" But no sooner had he uttered this lament than the answer came to him: "I thank God—through Jesus Christ our Lord!" (Romans 7:24–25). We are called upon to endure, to persevere in the race to the end, that we might attain the prize that never fades away—but we are also empowered by God Himself to accomplish this task. As long as we remain open to His correction, He will empower us to finish strong.

↶ Digging Deeper ↷

5. *How does a person forget God's law? How did this happen in Solomon's life? How does a Christian guard against this?*

6. *What does it mean to acknowledge God in all your ways? How is this done? Why is it important?*

7. *What does it mean to be wise in your own eyes? Give practical examples of this. How does it happen? How can one guard against it?*

8. When have you benefited from criticism? Was that criticism unpleasant to hear? What was required of you to submit to it?

ᕯ Taking It Personally ᕯ

9. What are you doing on a regular basis to ensure that you don't forget God's law? How can you improve your storehouse of knowledge?

10. Is the Lord calling you to correct some area of your Christian walk? What will you do this week to address that area?

WISDOM FROM ABOVE, WISDOM FROM BELOW

PROVERBS 1, 9, 14, 26; JAMES 3

∽ THEMATIC BACKGROUND ∼

We have studied many aspects of wisdom and folly, and we have seen the results of each. The difference between wisdom and folly is so striking and so self-evident, that one must wonder why anyone would ever choose to be a fool. What could possible make someone lead a life marked by foolishness? The answer is simple: we are all born foolish. True wisdom comes only from God, but every human being is born in sin, separated from God and devoid of wisdom. The only way for anyone to escape folly and find wisdom is to receive God's forgiveness through the gospel. This brings us into a relationship with the source of wisdom, and the Holy Spirit begins His work of transforming our lives.

But the world does not acknowledge God as the source of true wisdom; it has its own form of so-called wisdom to lull the simple into complacency. This false wisdom is a mere counterfeit of God's truth, yet on the surface it can seem like sound wisdom to those who lack understanding. This is a deadly deception, and even God's people can sometimes be fooled into embracing false wisdom.

The source of this worldly wisdom is the devil and his demons, and its purpose is to draw people away from God. Believers must be aware of the two types of wisdom—that from below and that from above—and be able to discern between them. That is the focus of our final study.

∽ READING PROVERBS 1:7–19 ∼

THE BEGINNING OF WISDOM: *Before a person can hope to gain wisdom, he must first learn a deep reverence for God, since God is the source of all genuine wisdom.*

7. THE FEAR OF THE LORD IS THE BEGINNING OF KNOWLEDGE: Here is a short summary of all that we have been studying concerning wisdom. God is the sole source of true wisdom, and wisdom can be attained only when one holds God in reverence as Lord and Savior.

FOOLS DESPISE WISDOM AND INSTRUCTION: "The fool has said in his heart, 'There is no God'" (Psalm 14:1)—and has cut himself off from the source of wisdom by doing so. The fool hates knowledge and correction; he is quick to argue (Proverbs 20:3) and just as quick to express anger (Proverbs 29:11); he is complacent (Proverbs 1:32), and he "trusts in his own heart" (Proverbs 28:26). All of these things represent the wisdom of the world.

10. IF SINNERS ENTICE YOU: The word translated *entice* means literally "to be open-minded, simple, gullible." The world works overtime to seduce our minds into gullibility. We must remain keenly aware that Satan is always trying to seduce us away from God. The world system offers a kind of wisdom, or what appears to be wisdom on the surface but is actually pseudo-wisdom, as we will see shortly. Worse, this "wisdom" is not a passive thing, like a choice between different brands in the grocery store; it is very active, used by the enemy of our souls to lead us astray.

STREET GANG: *Solomon gives us another vignette, this time of criminals enticing a youth to join them. He uses an extreme example to illustrate some common attitudes.*

11. COME WITH US: The fact is, most people do follow this invitation and wind up on the wide road. What these men neglect to mention when inviting others to follow is that the source of their wisdom is hell itself.

LET US LIE IN WAIT TO SHED BLOOD: At first reading, Solomon's example of robbery and murder seems extreme. After all, most of us are not invited by friends to go out on a mugging spree; such an enticement would be easy to resist. But James will show that this is exactly what we do when we envy our neighbors and when we set our own interests above the interests of others. The world's wisdom urges us to "look out for number one," but it is actually telling us to "lurk secretly for the innocent without cause."

12. SWALLOW THEM . . . WHOLE: Such bloodthirsty language seems outrageous, and most Christians would never believe themselves to be capable of such thinking. Yet James will suggest otherwise. When we follow the wisdom from below, this is precisely the way we end up thinking: other people become mere ends to our means, and we wind up biting and devouring one another.

13. ALL KINDS OF PRECIOUS POSSESSIONS: The wisdom of this world sets great value on material possessions, social status, leisure time, and so on—values that are constantly touted in our society today.

15. DO NOT WALK IN THE WAY WITH THEM: The more we walk in a certain direction, the more we develop a path. Walking on a path implies a consistent lifestyle, but there is only one path that leads to God. The best way to avoid sin is to avoid those people whose paths lead to sin. Christians should not keep company with fools.

17. IN VAIN THE NET IS SPREAD IN THE SIGHT OF ANY BIRD: That is, even a bird isn't caught in a net when it sees the trapper setting it up—yet the fool is! The fool sets a trap for the innocent, but he ends up falling into it himself.

19. GREEDY FOR GAIN: One facet of the wisdom from below is the idea that one must always be gaining more. This is a very unattractive quality, one that puts its possessor on the same level as a grave: "The leech has two daughters—Give and Give! There are three things that are never satisfied, four never say, 'Enough!': The grave, the barren womb, the earth that is not satisfied with water—and the fire never says, 'Enough!'" (Proverbs 30:15–16).

⟿ READING PROVERBS 9:1–18 ⟿

THE WOMAN WISDOM: *Solomon personifies wisdom as a woman who has built a house and prepared a banquet for any who will come inside.*

1. WISDOM HAS BUILT HER HOUSE: In an earlier study, we saw wisdom personified as a woman standing in the public square, inviting passersby to embrace her free gift. Now she is pictured at home, inside her spacious house. Both wisdom and folly have houses, however, and both invite the simple inside. This chapter will help us discern which house is the true home of the wisdom from above.

SHE HAS HEWN OUT HER SEVEN PILLARS: One notable difference between the two houses is that wisdom has built her own residence. God is the author and creator of all wisdom, while the world only offers a counterfeit. The seven pillars suggest perfection and completeness, as well as a sturdy security that cannot be shaken.

2. SHE HAS SLAUGHTERED HER MEAT: The woman personified as wisdom bears a striking resemblance to the wise woman of Proverbs 31. She is diligent and has prepared a great banquet for the simple who come to her—whereas the woman of folly idly sits around.

3. THE HIGHEST PLACES OF THE CITY: Both wisdom and folly are calling to the simple from the highest places of the city, very prominent and visible to all who pass by. This reminds us that there is a constant battle between the wisdom from above and the wisdom from below, as both seek the hearts and minds of mankind. Christians know the source of wisdom from above, and we are sealed in His love—yet we must still be on guard against the seductions of the world.

4. WHOEVER IS SIMPLE, LET HIM TURN IN HERE: Both wisdom and folly make the same offer, promising wisdom and knowledge within their homes. The wisdom of this age is a counterfeit, but at times it is a good counterfeit—it can be difficult for the simple to discern between the two. We need the timeless guidance of God to discern, and He provides that guidance to anyone who asks.

5. MY BREAD . . . THE WINE I HAVE MIXED: Wisdom offers true sustenance, which she has prepared by her own hand. Folly, by contrast, offers stolen food.

7. HE WHO CORRECTS A SCOFFER GETS SHAME FOR HIMSELF: That is, the scoffer responds with contempt and abuse when someone tries to correct him. As we saw in our previous study, the fool is wise in his own eyes and will not accept rebukes. This is another facet of the wisdom from below: "trust your instincts," "follow your heart," and so forth.

8. REBUKE A WISE MAN, AND HE WILL LOVE YOU: The wisdom from above, however, is humble and teachable, not wise in its own eyes but eager to become more like Christ.

12. YOU ARE WISE FOR YOURSELF: That is, your wisdom will benefit you. Each person chooses for himself whether he will be wise or a scoffer, and each person will reap the fruit of that choice.

THE WOMAN FOLLY: *We next meet another personification, this time a woman who represents folly. She seems similar to wisdom, but the difference is deadly.*

13. CLAMOROUS: Folly is now personified, as wisdom was previously. Wisdom, however, was diligent and industrious, preparing a healthy banquet for her guests; but folly is merely boisterous, saying nothing—because she knows nothing. As wisdom resembled the woman of Proverbs 31, so folly resembles the woman of Proverbs 7—the sexual fool.

14. SHE SITS AT THE DOOR OF HER HOUSE: Wisdom was hardworking, but folly is lazy. The sad fact is that she doesn't really need to exert much effort to seduce the simple, because mankind walks to folly naturally.

16. WHOEVER IS SIMPLE, LET HIM TURN IN HERE: Folly promises wisdom, but it is a phony wisdom that comes from below rather than above.

17. STOLEN WATER IS SWEET: That which is forbidden can seem all the more enticing simply because it is forbidden. This thinking originated with our first parents, Adam and Eve, in the garden of Eden (Genesis 3). Eve was seduced into taking the forbidden fruit because the serpent persuaded her that God was simply trying to cheat her out of her rightful due—and the human race has followed that foolish thinking ever since.

⌁ READING PROVERBS 14:6–9, 12–15 ⌁

LEARN FROM THE FOOL: *A wise man can learn wisdom by observing the foolish behavior of the world. But this lesson is best learned from a distance.*

6. A SCOFFER SEEKS WISDOM: The desire for wisdom is common to all mankind; everyone desires to live with skill, avoiding disaster and finding fulfillment. The scoffer cannot find it, however, because he has refused to fear the Lord and has rejected all correction.

KNOWLEDGE IS EASY TO HIM WHO UNDERSTANDS: Understanding is having insight into the character and ways of God; it is the ability to see life from His perspective. This can only come from a personal relationship with God, and that is only available through His Son, Jesus. Those who reject Christ deny themselves of ever finding wisdom.

7. GO FROM THE PRESENCE OF A FOOLISH MAN: Again, Christians are not to keep company with fools. One can discern a fool from his speech, as we saw in Study 7.

8. UNDERSTAND HIS WAY: The prudent person pays attention to the path that he is walking, and he learns from words of correction. The fool, by contrast, thinks that he is being prudent when he follows human wisdom, looking after his own interests and being wise in his own eyes. This is self-deception.

9. FOOLS MOCK AT SIN: The wisdom embraced by modern society teaches that sin is righteousness and righteousness is sin. The world today mocks the idea that immoral behavior is wrong, while simultaneously proclaiming that selfishness is a virtue.

12. THERE IS A WAY THAT SEEMS RIGHT TO A MAN: In today's culture, each man does that which is right in his own eyes, but that is the wisdom from below. The wisdom from above dictates that we must do what is right in God's eyes, regardless of what the world may think.

15. THE SIMPLE BELIEVES EVERY WORD: The world's wisdom is often absurd and even self-contradictory, yet many are still taken in. Fools are gullible because they have rejected the truth; therefore, they readily believe lies. They are like the blind who do not even know what they are stumbling over; they are spiritually blind because they have rejected the Light.

⌁ READING PROVERBS 26:7–12 ⌁

EATING VOMIT: *Fools may think themselves wise, but their folly prevents them from learning that they are fools. They return to their folly as a dog returns to its vomit.*

7. A PROVERB IN THE MOUTH OF FOOLS: The wisdom of man has many proverbs, which the world repeats to their own destruction: "God helps those who help themselves," "follow your heart," "love yourself," and so forth. Yet when one is faced with genuine hardship in life, those proverbs prove as crippled as a lame man's legs.

8. ONE WHO BINDS A STONE IN A SLING: Stones are placed loosely in a sling, they are not tied in place. A sling with a stone stuck in place is a useless weapon, just as a fool is useless in a position of authority. As the stone is intended to be cast out, so also is the fool.

9. A PROVERB IN THE MOUTH OF FOOLS: Here we see this phrase again. We just saw it in verse 7. Why did the writer repeat it? Clearly, he wanted to stress that even when a fool does learn words of wisdom, he still does not know how to use them correctly. He wields them wantonly, as a drunken man might swing a scourge of thorns. The result is only injury rather than healing, both to innocent bystanders and to himself.

11. AS A DOG RETURNS TO HIS OWN VOMIT: Dogs have the disconcerting and disgusting habit of consuming their own vomit. This vivid picture underscores the disgusting ways of the fool. His folly causes him harm, and he casts it off—only to return to it again and re-consume it. He cannot learn wisdom, because he has rejected its Source.

⤳ READING JAMES 3:13–17 ⤶

THE TWO WISDOMS: *James warns us that there are two forms of wisdom, one from below and one from above. True wisdom involves loving others.*

13. GOOD CONDUCT . . . MEEKNESS: The bottom-line is that true wisdom is moral; it produces holy conduct out of obedience to God's Word. Meekness is the opposite of self-promotion; it is the attitude of considering others better than yourself (see Philippians 2:3).

14. BITTER ENVY AND SELF-SEEKING: Prevailing wisdom teaches us to "keep up with the Joneses." This only causes us to covet and envy the things that others possess. It also teaches us to look after our own interests and let others take care of themselves. The self-seeking person is a self-promoter, someone who takes advantage of every opportunity to put himself forward. This runs contrary to meekness, an essential quality of the wisdom from on high.

15. EARTHLY, SENSUAL, DEMONIC: It is earthly and sensual wisdom because it encourages a person to focus on temporal issues, rather than to see life from God's perspective.

17. PEACEABLE, GENTLE: Notice that this list of godly qualities all center upon a person's interaction with other people. The wisdom from below teaches us to look after our own interests, but the wisdom from above encourages us to put others ahead of ourselves.

⌁ FIRST IMPRESSIONS ⌁

1. In what ways are Wisdom and Folly similar in Proverbs 9? In what ways are they different? How might a passerby have distinguished them?

2. How does one "[get] shame for himself" if he corrects a scoffer (Proverbs 9:7)? When have you experienced this? What principle does it demonstrate?

3. What does Folly mean when she says that "stolen water is sweet"? What principle of worldly wisdom does this illustrate? What does God's Word say?

4. *How does the world today illustrate the teaching that "the simple believes every word" (Proverbs 14:15)? Why is this so? What is the solution to this problem?*

⤳ Some Key Principles ⤳

Wisdom from below is wise in its own eyes.

The person who is wise in his own eyes has rejected the truths of God. He assumes that he can find things of lasting value in this world, and he gives little thought to eternity. This is precisely the behavior of those who embrace the wisdom from below. Such "wisdom" is intended to keep a person's focus on the things of earth, lest the fool stop and consider his ways, turn from his folly, and find wisdom and salvation from God.

It is this element of considering our ways that makes it so dangerous to become wise in our own eyes. The self-satisfied man considers himself to have already obtained knowledge and understanding, so he is not open to rebuke or correction. But if we harden our hearts and minds against correction, then we deafen our ears to the Lord's voice and become resistant to His gentle hand. We then place ourselves in the position of needing a stern rebuke and harsher discipline if we are to continue the race. Solomon gives us a picture of such a man, and he did not finish the race well.

By maintaining an eternal perspective, seeing ourselves and the world through God's eyes rather than man's, we remain humble and open to correction. Isaiah warned, "Woe to those who call evil good, and good evil; who put darkness for light, and light for darkness; who put bitter for sweet, and sweet for bitter! Woe to those who are wise in their own eyes, and prudent in their own sight!" (Isaiah 5:20–21). Only when we exchange such arrogance for humility before God will He ensure that we finish the race well.

True wisdom only comes through the gospel.

Today's society cites many axioms that purport to be wisdom: "follow your heart," "love yourself," and "to thine own self be true." But all of this so-called wisdom is absent the basis of wisdom: God's love for the world seen through the death and resurrection of his Son. When we are lost in our sin, we know neither wisdom nor the author of wisdom. Instead, we believe lies about the world, and we think those lies are the embodiment of wisdom.

But such wisdom is not from above. Rather, true wisdom comes from having a heart transformed by God's Spirit and then having eyes that are opened to the truth in God's Word. For this reason, it is absolutely impossible for those who are apart from Christ to have any semblance of true wisdom. "For the wisdom of this world is foolishness with God" (1 Corinthians 3:19). At the center of the two wisdoms stands the cross. To those who are apart from Christ, the cross represents supreme foolishness. The world assumes that if Jesus were really God, the last thing he would do is die on the cross. But for those who are being saved, the cross shows the true power and wisdom of God.

Do not keep company with fools.

Proverbs warns us that we tend to become like the people we spend the most time with. This can be both positive and negative. On one hand, we can grow more wise if we spend time with those who walk in wisdom; on the other hand, we can become angry if we hang around angry people (Proverbs 22:24–25). If our close friends are fools, we will eventually begin to imitate them—and become foolish ourselves.

This does not mean that a Christian should never reach out to the lost; we were all fools once, yet God reached out to save us. There is a place for evangelism, but not among our intimate circle of closest friends. It is important for Christians to be in regular fellowship with other like-minded believers because it deepens our faith and provides role models who can influence us toward godliness. The writer of Hebrews urged us to "consider one another in order to stir up love and good works, not forsaking the assembling of ourselves together, as is the manner of some, but exhorting one another, and so much the more as you see the Day approaching" (10:24–25).

Those who want to grow in wisdom make it a point to keep company with the wise; those who keep company with fools will begin to imitate them. It is proper to share the gospel with the lost, but we must not become friends with the world in the process. "Friendship with the world is enmity with God," warned the apostle James. "Whoever therefore wants to be a friend of the world makes himself an enemy of God" (James 4:4).

5.   Why are we commanded to "go from the presence of a foolish man" (Proverbs 14:7)? What is the danger of keeping company with a fool? How does a Christian balance this with evangelism?

6.   What is "self-seeking"? Give some practical examples. How is this different from true wisdom? Why does wisdom require that we treat others as better than ourselves?

7.   List below some key differences between wisdom from below and wisdom from above.

8.   Define the following adjectives that describe heavenly wisdom, giving examples of each.
Pure:

Peaceable:

Gentle:

Willing to yield:

Mercy:

Without partiality:

Without hypocrisy:

ꝃ Taking It Personally ꝃ

9. Do you tend to put others ahead of yourself? When do you find yourself doing the reverse? In what areas might the Lord be calling you to greater selflessness?

10. Is your intimate circle of friends characterized by wisdom or folly? Whom do you find yourself imitating in daily life? How can you imitate Christ more closely?

SECTION 4:

SUMMARY

Notes and Prayer Requests

⟿ 12 ⟿

REVIEWING KEY PRINCIPLES

⌇ LOOKING BACK ⌇

Over the course of these studies, we have examined the life of Solomon, the "wisest man who ever lived." In so doing, we have gained a deeper understanding of God's great gift of wisdom, which comes only through believing in his Son, Jesus Christ. Throughout these studies, we have gotten to know quite a number of interesting characters, including those who exhibited wisdom and others who lived in folly. One theme has remained constant throughout these studies: *God is faithful*, and those who obey Him will grow in faithfulness as well.

One who would be wise must first and foremost have a deep reverence for the character and commands of God, for this is the foundation of all true wisdom. Such a person is open to correction and will work constantly to know God and obey His commands. But the world also offers a counterfeit form of wisdom, and Christians must always be on guard to avoid being misled by this "wisdom from below."

Following are a few of the major principles we have found as we have examined God's Word in these studies. There are many more that we don't have room to reiterate, so take some time to review the earlier studies—or better still, to meditate on the Scripture passages that we have covered. Ask the Holy Spirit to give you wisdom and insight into His Word. He will not refuse.

⌇ SOME KEY PRINCIPLES ⌇

The Lord does not tolerate syncretism.

Syncretism is the act of combining elements of diverse religious philosophies into a new form of worship. Solomon attempted to do this when he added pagan practices to the prescribed worship of God, drawing in elements from the worship of a wide variety of false gods. The Lord had expressly forbidden His people from intermarrying for that very reason, and Solomon's paganism led to the loss of his kingdom.

The modern church has frequently fallen into syncretism as well, incorporating worldly principles and ideas into the Word of God. This can be seen in the addition of

New Age ideas, evolutionary thinking, self-help approaches to sinful behaviors, or pandering to cultural trends. Christians are very unwise when they attempt to add to the written Word of God, because it is complete already, as pertinent today as when it was written.

As we will see in the course of these studies, the world offers a form of wisdom that can appear sound at first glance, but its source is not from God. This "wisdom" is from below, not from above. Christians must be constantly on guard to prevent such false wisdom from being added to the sound teachings of Scripture.

Parents should deliberately teach their children in the ways of wisdom.

Wisdom does not come naturally to children—quite the contrary, in fact. Proverbs tells us that "foolishness is bound up in the heart of a child" (22:15), reminding us that all humans are born sinners and foolish behavior comes naturally to us all. This same verse, however, teaches us to replace a child's folly with wisdom by using "the rod of correction."

The "rod of correction" includes far more than corporal punishment, however. David imparted wisdom to Solomon by teaching him from God's law. He also modeled wisdom for his son, demonstrating by his own lifestyle what it meant to be a man after God's own heart. This did not mean that David was perfect; the Bible records some grievous sins in his life, including, as mentioned previously, his early relations with Bathsheba, who came to be Solomon's mother.

No Christian parent is perfect; we all wrestle with our own sin, and so we all make bad decisions from time to time. Yet David's success in teaching wisdom to his son demonstrates that God uses sinners to teach other sinners His ways. This is especially true of parents and their children, and God's Word makes it clear that parents have a responsibility to train up their children in the ways of wisdom. "And these words which I command you today shall be in your heart. You shall teach them diligently to your children, and shall talk of them when you sit in your house, when you walk by the way, when you lie down, and when you rise up" (Deuteronomy 6:6–7).

Our words affect our actions and the actions of others.

Life seems to be filled with talk. The media bombards us with words; politicians prate ceaselessly about the economy and social affairs; people debate their opinions about everything under the sun. "It's all just words," we'll say, implying that words without action have no meaning.

But the Scriptures teach us that our words have a powerful effect, both on ourselves and on others. James used the illustration of a wildfire to indicate the destruction that can be caused by idle or careless speech. It can burn the person who utters it and scald the person who hears it. It can also spread its destruction in a wide circle, as one person's words are repeated by another. Each speaker's utterances lead to actions by himself or those around him.

This principle can also work in a positive way, however. As we learn to speak words of wisdom, we increase the likelihood that we will act in wisdom, and we encourage others to live in godliness. Consider James's analogy of a ship under the power of the wind: the pilot guides the rudder, and the rudder steers the whole ship. When we submit to the guidance of the Holy Spirit, He guides us in the use of our tongues, and our tongues can steer our lives into Christlike character.

The love of money is a sin.

The sluggard may work hard to avoid work, but when he's got work, he doesn't like to work hard at doing it. Wealth is always appealing, but the effort required to gain it is not. Consequently, the sluggard is easily susceptible to the sin of loving money.

Paul writes that "the love of money is a root of all kinds of evil" (1 Timothy 6:10). This is because it causes people to become more obsessed with the things of this world and less passionate about the things of God. When someone loves money, they become stingy and they close their hand to the poor. They make decisions based on finances rather than on God's will. They forget that the riches this world offers are of no value in eternity. This is why Jesus said, "You cannot serve both God and money" (Luke 16:13, NIV).

This principle applies also to the daily work that the Lord has provided for each of us. A job is a gift from the Lord, and it is also a ministry that He expects us to perform to the best of our abilities—working as unto Him, not our earthly masters (Ephesians 6:5–8). As Solomon reminds us, "Whatever your hand finds to do, do it with your might; for there is no work or device or knowledge or wisdom in the grave where you are going" (Ecclesiastes 9:10).

The wise person protects his purity as a precious treasure.

Our culture scorns the concept of chastity. Those who remain virgins until marriage are considered odd misfits, old-fashioned fuddy-duddies, even deviants of sorts. In the eyes of the world, promiscuous sex is considered healthy, a normal part of growing up, an inherent right of every individual, and as sacred as though it were guaranteed by the Constitution.

But God's Word teaches us that sexual purity is a precious treasure, something we should guard as carefully as we guard our eyesight. Solomon makes it clear that the wise person fights against the lusts of the flesh, while the fool gives into sexual immorality. Because healthy sexual intimacy is found *only* within the parameters of marriage, in that setting it is a great blessing to God's people.

It is obvious that sexual sin has a unique power to destroy a person's life. It is the sin that brought David down, as he slept with Solomon's mother, Bathsheba. It was the sin that first attacked the early church (see 1 Corinthians 5:19; Acts 15:20), and it is perhaps the most prevalent sin in our culture today. Paul taught us that sexual sin is so unique, that when we sin sexually, we sin against the Holy Spirit Himself. "Flee sexual immorality," wrote Paul. "Every sin that a man does is outside the body, but he who commits sexual immorality sins against his own body. Or do you not know that your body is the temple of the Holy Spirit who is in you, whom you have from God, and you are not your own? For you were bought at a price; therefore glorify God in your body and in your spirit, which are God's" (1 Corinthians 6:18–20).

The Lord uses rebuke and correction to keep us running the race.

Nobody likes to be criticized, and it can be very painful to be reprimanded. Even basic correction can be difficult to endure, especially when it is done in a harsh or demeaning manner. We've all encountered people who seem to delight in finding fault with others, and it is hard to see any value in such constant words of criticism.

Yet every athlete understands the importance of criticism. Criticism exposes weakness, which when corrected makes an athlete perform better. If an athlete ignores his coach, he is only hurting his own performance.

The same principle holds true in the Christian life. None of us is perfect, and we all fall short of the completed image of Christ. Like the athlete, we all have areas that need to be strengthened, and the sinful nature is constantly fighting to reassert itself—even in areas where we've gained victory in the past. That's why it is so important that we receive the Lord's corrections with a teachable spirit; as Jesus stated, "As many as I love, I rebuke and chasten. Therefore be zealous and repent" (Revelation 3:19).

We do not run the race alone or under our own power.

The world of athletic competition features some amazing accomplishments. Runners have set world records for speed; mountain climbers demonstrate incredible endurance; skydivers defy death by leaping from great heights—there are countless feats of prowess being undertaken by daring men and women all over the world every day. But there is one thing that all these feats have in common: they are within the realm of possibility for human endeavor.

That is not the case when it comes to the Christian race. We are called to be like Christ, but there is no person on earth who can accomplish that feat on his own power. We are all born under the curse of sin, and none of us can overcome that curse. Left to our own devices, no one could hope to live as Christ lived, for He was without sin. Thank God we are not left to our own devices!

God has given His Spirit to each believer—the very same Spirit that raised Christ from the dead (Romans 8:11)—and it is through His power and guidance that we overcome the sinful nature that holds us captive. Paul once cried, "O wretched man that I am! Who will deliver me from this body of death?" But no sooner had he uttered this lament than the answer came to him: "I thank God—through Jesus Christ our Lord!" (Romans 7:24–25). We are called upon to endure, to persevere in the race to the end, that we might attain the prize that never fades away—but we are also empowered by God Himself to accomplish this task. As long as we remain open to His correction, He will empower us to finish strong.

True wisdom only comes through the gospel.

Today's society cites many axioms that purport to be wisdom: "follow your heart," "love yourself," and "to thine own self be true." But all of this so-called wisdom is absent the basis of wisdom: God's love for the world seen through the death and resurrection of his Son. When we are lost in our sin, we know neither wisdom nor the author of wisdom. Instead, we believe lies about the world, and we think those lies are the embodiment of wisdom.

But such wisdom is not from above. Rather, true wisdom comes from having a heart transformed by God's Spirit and then having eyes that are opened to the truth in God's Word. For this reason, it is absolutely impossible for those who are apart from Christ to have any semblance of true wisdom. "For the wisdom of this world is foolishness with God" (1 Corinthians 3:19). At the center of the two wisdoms stands the cross. To those who are apart from Christ, the cross represents supreme foolishness. The world assumes that if Jesus were really God, the last thing he would do is die on the cross. But for those who are being saved, the cross shows the true power and wisdom of God.

Do not keep company with fools.

Proverbs warns us that we tend to become like the people we spend the most time with. This can be both positive and negative. On one hand, we can grow more wise if we spend time with those who walk in wisdom; on the other hand, we can become angry if we hang around angry people (Proverbs 22:24–25). If our close friends are fools, we will eventually begin to imitate them—and become foolish ourselves.

This does not mean that a Christian should never reach out to the lost; we were all fools once, yet God reached out to save us. There is a place for evangelism, but not among our intimate circle of closest friends. It is important for Christians to be in regular fellowship with other like-minded believers because it deepens our faith and provides role models who can influence us toward godliness. The writer of Hebrews urged us to "consider one another in order to stir up love and good works, not forsaking the assembling of ourselves together, as is the manner of some, but exhorting one another, and so much the more as you see the Day approaching" (10:24–25).

Those who want to grow in wisdom make it a point to keep company with the wise; those who keep company with fools will begin to imitate them. It is proper to share the gospel with the lost, but we must not become friends with the world in the process. "Friendship with the world is enmity with God," warned the apostle James. "Whoever therefore wants to be a friend of the world makes himself an enemy of God" (James 4:4).

⤳ Digging Deeper ⤳

1. *What are some of the more important things you have learned from the wisdom writings of Solomon?*

2. *Which of the concepts or principles have you found most encouraging? Which have been most challenging?*

3. *What aspects of "walking with God" are you already doing in your life? Which areas need strengthening?*

4. *Which of the characters we've studied have you felt the most drawn to? How might you emulate that person in your own life?*

⤣ TAKING IT PERSONALLY ⤢

5. *Have you taken a definite stand for Jesus Christ? Have you accepted His free gift of salvation? If not, what is preventing you?*

6. What areas of your personal life have been most convicted during this study? What exact things will you do to address these convictions? Be specific.

7. What have you learned about the character of God during this study? How has this insight affected your worship or prayer life?

8. List below the specific things you want to see God do in your life in the coming month. List also the things that you intend to change in your own life in that time. Return to this list in one month, and hold yourself accountable to fulfill these things.

If you would like to continue in your study of the Old Testament, read the next title in this series, *A House Divided*, or the previous title, *The Restoration of a Sinner*.